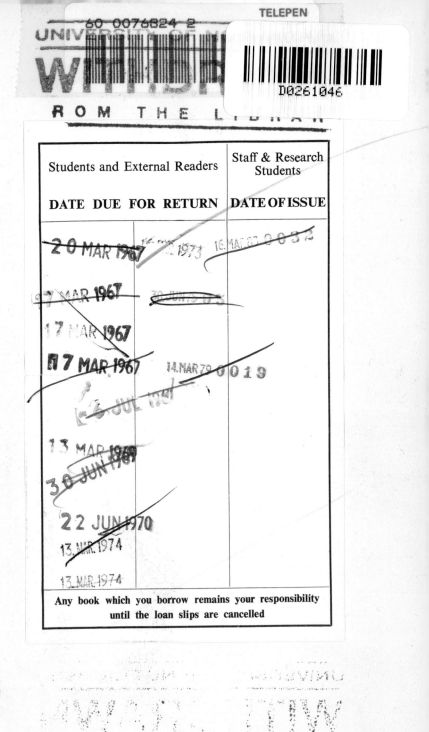

Students and External Readers	Staff & Research Students
DATE DUE FOR RETURN	**DATE OF ISSUE**
20 MAR 1967	1973 16. MAR 87
17 MAR 1967	30 JUN 79
17 MAR 1967	
17 MAR 1967	14.MAR 79 0019
-6 JUL	
13 MAR 1967	
30 JUN 1967	
22 JUN 1970	
13. MAR 1974	
13. MAR 1974	

Any book which you borrow remains your responsibility until the loan slips are cancelled

ST. ANTONY'S PAPERS · NUMBER I

★

SOVIET AFFAIRS

NUMBER ONE

ST. ANTONY'S PAPERS · NUMBER I

SOVIET AFFAIRS

Number One

1956

CHATTO & WINDUS

LONDON

PUBLISHED BY
CHATTO AND WINDUS LTD
42 WILLIAM IV STREET
LONDON WC2

★

CLARKE, IRWIN AND CO LTD
TORONTO

PRINTED IN GREAT BRITAIN BY
ROBERT CUNNINGHAM AND SONS LTD, ALVA

CONTENTS

CONTENTS

The main emphasis of the work at St. Antony's College Oxford since its foundation in 1950 has been in the fields of modern history and international affairs. The College organizes a number of regular Seminars at which are read papers produced by its members in the course of their research or by visiting experts from other institutions. The College further sponsors the delivery of lectures in Oxford by scholars of international reputation in their respective fields.

An appreciable volume of contribution to scholarship is thus being produced under the auspices of St. Antony's, and the present series has been started in order to preserve and present a selection of this work. The series is not, however, confined to this material alone and includes contributions from other places.

Three numbers a year are issued and each number is devoted to a particular topic or a particular part of the world.

THE CHEKA

By E. J. Scott

THIS paper attempts to assemble the available evidence concerning the origin and early development of the Soviet political police. The difficulties here arise not only from the secret nature of the organisation, but from the great efforts which have been made to construct a false image of it for propaganda purposes. Misrepresentation of the police seems to have followed closely after misrepresentation of the Bolshevik Party among the very first tasks of Soviet internal propaganda. The task was well begun under Lenin. Stalin can only be credited with its simplification, by restricting all accounts of the police to a few lines and by concentrating all State historical archives in their hands.

The latest and briefest account of the police, contained in the second edition of the Soviet Encyclopaedia (Volume 9, 1951), gives as its origin a Decree of Sovnarcom of December 20, 1917, which is said to have established the Cheka. The Decree is alleged to have been adopted on Lenin's initiative and to have been based on a note he wrote to Dzerzhinsky, who was appointed head of the organization. The reason for its establishment is said to have been the discovery soon after the Bolshevik revolution of counter-revolutionary plots financed by foreign and Russian capitalists.

Though Lenin is claimed to have founded the Cheka, no evidence has ever been brought forward showing how or when he did so. His note to Dzerzhinsky, on which a Decree organizing the Cheka is said to have been based, is in fact concerned only with drafting measures for conscripting bourgeois labour, and has no reference to an organization such as the Cheka. Nevertheless, Soviet commentators have found it expedient to link the founding of the Cheka to this particular note for the sake of its 'quotable' preamble, in which Lenin pictured the chaos in Petrograd as the product of unscrupulous attempts by class-enemy 'counter-revolutionaries' and 'saboteurs' to 'undermine the government', and declared the necessity of 'extraordinary measures' to combat them.[1]

[1] The note was first published in *Krasnyi Arkhiv*, Vol. 5 (1924). It is also con-

Whether or not Lenin played a direct part in establishing the Cheka, he had long been supplying, in his writings on the theory and tactics of revolution, the theoretical arguments which were used to justify its creation. He had, in particular, proclaimed that the successful consummation of a proletarian revolution depended on the effectiveness with which the resistance of counter-revolutionary classes in the period following the seizure of power was smashed under a dictatorship of the proletariat. In 1908 he had, for example, asserted that the Paris Commune of 1871, 'the first proletarian government', had not endured because it had not followed up its initial victory with a ruthless destruction of the counter-revolutionaries.[2] Already in 1905 he had envisaged the use of terror in the style of the French Jacobins of 1793, 'to settle accounts with Tsarism' after the revolution.[3] It was allegedly in accordance with this Leninist theory that, as Pokrovsky later put it, the Cheka 'sprang from the very essence of the proletarian revolution', and that the terror was 'the inevitable consequence' of that revolution.[4]

The Petrograd Military-Revolutionary Committee, which carried out the seizure of power, numbered among its tasks immediately after the revolution 'the fighting of counter-revolution', and organized a security department for this purpose.[5] Dzerzhinsky, who from the very first was engaged in security work, proposed to the Committee, on December 4, the organization of a special commission to fight counter-revolution.[6]

tained in Lenin's *Collected Works* (third Russian edition, Vol. 22, pp. 126-9). Only the first part of the note is normally quoted in Soviet accounts of the founding of the Cheka.

[2] Lenin, *op. cit.*, Vol. 12, p. 163.

[3] Lenin, *op. cit.*, Vol. 8, p. 64 ('Two Tactics'), and Vol. 7, p. 270. According to Bonch-Bruyevich (*Na boyevikh postakh fevralskoi i oktyabrskoi revolyutsii* (1930), pp. 197-8), the Jacobin Reign of Terror exerted a strong influence in shaping Bolshevik ideas on the terror: 'We were well acquainted with the dimensions of the red terror during that great fight (the French Revolution). We were all long ago mentally prepared for the period when we would have to defend the achievements of the dictatorship of the proletariat . . . by using one of the most radical and effective means of our revolutionary struggle—the red terror.' Dzerzhinsky was described by Bukharin and others as 'a real proletarian Jacobin' (*F. Dzerzhinsky, sbornik statei* (1931), p. 141), and, according to Herriot (*La Russie Nouvelle* (1922), pp. 183-5) he was 'a Slav Saint-Just'. Stalin (*Collected Works* in Russian, Vol. 10, p. 234) claimed that the Cheka was 'more or less analogous' to the Comité de Salut public. But parallels between the Bolshevik and the Jacobin terror were developed in order to fit the Marxist historical scheme. (See, for example, the comparative analysis of the two terrors in *Entsiklopediya Gosudarstva i Prava* (1925-7), Article: 'Terror'.)

[4] *Pravda*, December 18, 1927.

[5] *Istoriya Grazhdanskoi Voini* (1943), Vol. 2, pp. 589-91.

[6] *Sovetskoye Administrativnoye Pravo* (1946), p. 184. Kozhevnikov, *Istoriya Sovetskogo Suda 1917-1947* (1948), p. 59.

One may suspect that his objective was to reconstruct the security department on broader lines so that it covered not only Petrograd but all Soviet-held territory, and to regularize its position so far as possible in the apparatus on the new administration. It was apparently as a result of Dzerzhinsky's proposal that the Cheka was organized, and was prepared to take over its duties on December 21 after being approved by Sovnarcom on the 20th.

The establishment of the Cheka was first announced on December 26, when the *Gazette of the Provisional Worker-Peasant Government* published the following statement on a page devoted to minor announcements: 'By decision of Sovnarcom of December 7, (20th, new style), the All-Russian Extraordinary Commission for fighting counter-revolution and sabotage, attached to Sovnarcom, has been formed. The Commission is situated at No. 2 Gorokhovaya. Receiving hours: 12 till 5 o'clock.' No Decree establishing the Cheka was ever published by the Press or in the *Collection of Laws of the R.S.F.S.R.*[7] However, what seems to be an extract from a hastily written minute of Sovnarcom's decision approving the organization was first reproduced in the reminiscences[8] of a prominent Chekist, Latsis, in 1926, and then in an article[9] on the history of the police by Pokrovsky in 1927. While Pokrovsky admitted that the decision was not a Decree and that Lenin's note to Dzerzhinsky had no direct bearing on it, he was so successful in exaggerating[10] the significance of these two documents, that later commentators have not scrupled to attribute to the decision the full status of a Decree and to the note the character of a basic directive for the founding of the Cheka.

The statutes of the Cheka, which do appear in the *Collection of Laws*, were not drawn up until November 1918.[11] They declared that it was an organ of Sovnarcom, which appointed the members of its central collegium, and that it worked in

[7] The Chekist, Moroz, writing in *Pravda* of January 31, 1919, stated: 'The existence of the Chekas was not provided for by any legal basis . . . life itself dictated that they should be organized.'

[8] *Proletarskaya Revolyutsiya*, 9(56), (1926), pp. 81-97.

[9] *Pravda*, December 18, 1927.

[10] According to Bertrand Wolfe (*Foreign Affairs*, October 1952, p. 42), Pokrovsky 'held to professional standards, had regard for documents and evidence, though at times he wrestled mightily with them to yield what he sought.' This verdict on Pokrovsky is far too complimentary. There are at least two deliberately false statements in his article on the police:
(1) 'Only in September 1918 did Sovnarcom order everyone in contact with White Guards to be shot.'
(2) 'Before July 1918 the Cheka only shot bandits and provocateurs, not counter-revolutionaries.' [11] *R.S.F.S.R. Laws* (1918), 80: 842.

3

close contact with the Commissariats of Justice and Internal Affairs (N.K.V.D.). They also recognized the right of Ve Cheka (the 'All-Russian', central Cheka) and the local Chekas to organize armed detachments of troops. But they did not attempt to define the exact functions or powers of the police; Lenin only recommended that this should be done in December 1921 just before the Cheka was transformed into the G.P.U.

The Cheka apparatus developed not only on a territorial basis, in each local administrative centre, but on 'functional' lines, in those organizations, such as the transport system and the armed forces, on whose reliable functioning the security of the regime appeared most to depend. This process began early in 1918, but not until the middle of the year were serious attempts made (by calling an 'All-Russian Conference of Chekas', and by issuing instructions on the organizational pattern to be followed) to co-ordinate it from the centre.

In March 1918 the local Soviets were requested to organize Chekas in the 'Guberniyas' and 'Uyezds', and were informed that henceforward only the Chekas were to have the right to carry out arrests and other measures in the fight against 'counter-revolutionaries'.[12] The chairmen and members of the Chekas were to be elected by the Soviets with the subsequent approval of Ve Cheka. Higher level Chekas were empowered to send their representatives to lower level ones, where their vote was decisive, and to reverse the decisions of the lower Chekas.[13] As Bolshevik power established itself beyond the R.S.F.S.R., in the Ukraine, Central Asia and the Caucasus, Chekas were formed in these areas on the same lines as the All-Russian Cheka. One of the first established non-Russian Chekas was the All-Ukrainian Cheka, which at the end of November 1918 was attached to the Ukrainian 'Department of Internal Affairs'.[14]

The formation of 'functional' Chekas began in May 1918

[12] A Decree of 16(29) December 1917, signed by the Commissar of Justice, Steinberg, had authorized the following to order arrests:
(a) investigation organs attached to the Petrograd Soviet;
(b) similar organs attached to local Soviets;
(c) Revolutionary Tribunals;
(d) 'the All-Russian investigation Commission' (the Cheka);
(e) the Commission for fighting pogroms. (*R.S.F.S.R. Laws* (1917), 9: 145.)

[13] *Izvestiya*, March 22, 1918. *R.S.F.S.R. Laws* (1918), 80: 842. 66: 728.
There seems to have been an even earlier attempt to form local Chekas in the Soviets to combat speculation. (*Gazeta Vremennogo Raboche-Krestyanskogo Pravitelstva*, December 19, 1917 (January 1, 1918).)

[14] Kozhevnikov, *op. cit.*, p. 90.
L. Bach, *Le Droit et les institutions de la Russie Soviétique* (Paris, 1923), p. 152, gives December 3, 1918, as the date for the establishment of the Ukrainian Cheka.

when the control of frontier areas was taken over by special frontier Chekas. In July and September, railway and post and telegraph departments were set up in local Chekas. Transport Chekas ('Te Chekas') were attached to the most important river and rail communication centres.[15] Already in November 1918 the Chekist Moroz declared: 'There is no sphere of our life where the Cheka does not have its eagle eye.'[16]

In February 1919 the task of 'combating counter-revolution and espionage' in the army and fleet was given to a 'Special Department' ('Osobi Otdel') of Ve Cheka with subordinate 'special departments' attached to military units and with its agents in foreign territory.[17] The danger of 'counter-revolution' in the armed forces lay not so much in the possible treachery of former Tsarist officers and representatives of the 'counter-revolutionary classes' employed as 'specialists', as in the unreliability and demoralization of the peasant-soldiers. The first task of the 'special departments' seems to have been to attempt to forestall mass desertions and, by employing terroristic methods, to help build up discipline throughout the Red Army. Through the 'special departments', the Cheka during the civil war came to exercise what appeared to be supreme authority over large territories.[18] A resolution[19] of the 8th Party Congress in March 1919 declared that the local 'special departments' were subordinated to the political commissars of Armies and Fronts, while their general direction and control was exercised by Ve Cheka. But by 1921, according to Latsis,[20] the 'special departments' were no longer dependent on the political commissars or the Revolutionary-Military Council headed by Trotsky.

Already in March 1918 all newspapers had been obliged to send three copies of each issue to Cheka headquarters for censorship. Failure to do so was punishable by the closing down of the paper.[21] By the end of 1918 the Cheka had developed a system of concentration camps for political prisoners quite distinct from the ordinary prisons maintained by the Commissariat of Justice. In April 1919 the Chekas were ordered to establish forced labour camps, which were subsequently controlled by the N.K.V.D. through the local Soviets.[22]

[15] Kozhevnikov, *op. cit.*, p. 60. [16] *Izvestiya*, November 6, 1918.
[17] *R.S.F.S.R. Laws* (1919), 6: 58.
[18] *Report of the Committee to collect information on Russia* (1921), [Cmd. 1240], p. 41, contains the testimony of a British officer in Siberia and a Vice-Consul in Baku concerning the powers of the 'Special departments'.
[19] 'Spravochnik partinogo rabotnika', *Vypusk* 1, 1921, p. 23.
[20] Latsis, *Chrezvychainiye Komissii po borbe s kontrrevolyutsiei* (1921), pp. 26-30.
[21] *Izvestiya*, March 27, 1918.
[22] *R.S.F.S.R. Laws* (1919), 12: 124.

The Sovnarcom decision of December 20, 1917, formulated the tasks of the Cheka as follows:

(1) 'To investigate and liquidate all attempts or actions connected with counter-revolution or sabotage, no matter from whom they may come, throughout Russia.

(2) The handing over for trial by Revolutionary Tribunal of all saboteurs and counter-revolutionaries, and the elaboration of measures to fight them.

(3) The Commission carries out only a preliminary investigation in so far as this is necessary for preventive purposes.'

From the most imprecise terms of this decision it would seem that the Cheka was originally intended only to carry out investigations and to impose no stronger penalty than imprisonment. But the decision was, as we have pointed out, unpublished till the late twenties when it began to appear in 'improved' histories of the police. There is no reason to suppose that it ever guided the Cheka's actions, or to doubt that the necessity for the Cheka to employ terroristic methods had been envisaged from the start.

Though the terror was first openly proclaimed in September 1918, it was officially encouraged on a mass scale already in June, and the Bolsheviks had had recourse to it on critical occasions since the beginning of the year. Terroristic methods were employed to keep order in Petrograd even before the appearance of the Cheka. The 'special committee for fighting pogroms' which was set up on December 17, declared Petrograd in a state of siege and announced that 'attempts to break into wine-cellars, warehouses, factories, stalls, shops, private apartments, and so on and so forth, will be broken up by machine-gun fire without any kind of warning.'[23] Spontaneous outbreaks of terror directed against the former 'upper classes' were particularly widespread in the provinces; if local Bolsheviks did not encourage them they were helpless to prevent them.[24] The Left Social Revolutionary Commissar of Justice, Steinberg, later maintained that the Bolshevik announcement of December

[23] *Izvestiya*, December 6(19), 1917; and Bonch Bruyevich, p. 191.
This appears to be the first official reference to shootings by the Bolsheviks since the abolition of the death penalty was announced on November 10, 1917 (*R.S.F.S.R. Laws* (1917), 1: 4).

[24] The Commissar of Justice in Penza reported in April 1918: 'The mob-justice which is exercised in the Guberniya is most regrettable; outbreaks of mob-justice are not isolated, for in certain cases they have taken on the character of a mass epidemic, and with the legal apparatus as it is, there are absolutely no means, except military force, of fighting them.'
'Materiali N.K. Yustitsii', *Vypusk* I (1918), p. 24.

13 branding the entire Cadet Party as 'enemies of the people' had invited such incidents of mob justice as the murder of the Cadet ex-Ministers Kokoshkin and Shingarev in a Petrograd hospital by a band of sailors on January 20.[25] Lenin told the Petrograd Soviet on November 18, 1917: 'We are reproached with using terror, but we are not using the kind of terror used by the French revolutionaries who guillotined defenceless people, and I hope we will not, for we have strength with us.'[26] On December 15 it was Trotsky who told the same audience: 'During the French Revolution the Jacobins brought more honourable persons (than the Cadets) to the guillotine for resisting the people. We have not executed anyone and are not preparing to, but there are moments of popular fury and the Cadets are bringing it upon themselves. They are sabotaging and wrecking, and in every way intentionally aggravating the disorder, and not one of us will undertake to say that the people, if pushed to the extreme, will refrain from this final measure. But we are strong and we do not require such extremes. But everyone should know that the people will not be patient for long and will sweep away the obstacles from its path.'[27] Finally, on January 27, the Presidium of the Soviet heard Lenin, in the course of an address on the food shortage, declare: 'We can achieve nothing unless we use terror, and shoot speculators on the spot.'[28]

On February 23, 1918, immediately after the breaking off of the Brest Litovsk negotiations and the resumption of the German advance, an announcement was published by *Pravda* that the Cheka could 'see no other methods of fighting counter-revolutionaries, spies, speculators, looters, hooligans, saboteurs, and other parasites, than their merciless destruction on the spot'. Anyone attempting to flee from the capital would also be shot on the spot by Cheka detachments.[29] On the next day the first

---

[25] J. Steinberg, *Nravstvennyi lik revolyutsii* Berlin (1923), pp. 30-33.

On November 26 (December 9), 1917, the *Gazeta Vremennogo . . . Pravitelstva* had published a Decree (*R.S.F.S.R. Laws*, 1917, 4: 53) which declared that the Central Committee of the Cadet Party was the 'political staff' of a counter-revolutionary uprising whose leaders were 'outside the law'. Two more Decrees (*R.S.F.S.R. Laws*, 1917, 4: 64; 5: 70) were published on November 30 (December 13) which repeated the allegations against the Cadets in even stronger terms and announced that the Party was responsible for opening a civil war, and that it consisted of enemies of the people who were subject to arrest and to sentence by Revolutionary Tribunal.   [26] Lenin, *op. cit.*, Vol. 22, p. 50.

[27] *Izvestiya*, December 6, 1917.   [28] Lenin, *op. cit.*, Vol. 22, p. 243.

[29] *Dokumenti po istorii grazhdanskoi voini v S.S.S.R.*, edited by Mintz and Gorodetsky, Vol. I (1941), p. 49. On the preceding day *Pravda* had published the proclamation entitled: 'The Socialist Fatherland is in danger!' Shootings on the spot were also carried out by Red Army units in Petrograd under the command of a special military staff. (Bonch Bruyevich, pp. 274-6.)

reported case took place of the Cheka shooting without trial. The victim was a certain Prince Eboli, who, according to accounts by Latsis and his colleague Peters, had been 'masquerading as a Chekist' with forged papers in order to extort money. When the L.S.R. Party protested about the shooting Lenin, according to Latsis, would not allow the question to be put on the agenda of Sovnarcom.[30]

After the murder of Volodarsky on June 20 Lenin instructed Zinoviev that the terror should be applied more ruthlessly in Petrograd.[31] The final break with the L.S.R. Party after their murder of Mirbach (July 6), and risings organized by Savinkov at Yaroslavl, Rybinsk and Murom(July 6-21), further increased the slaughter.[32] Early in June, Dzerzhinsky granted a press interview[33] in which he described the character of the Cheka as follows: 'We stand for organized terror.... Terror is an absolute necessity during times of revolution.... We terrorize the enemies of the Soviet government in order to stop crime at its inception.... When confronted with evidence criminals almost in every case confess; and what argument can have greater weight than a criminal's own confession? ... The Cheka is not a court. The Cheka is the defence of the revolution as the Red Army is. And just as in the civil war the Red Army cannot stop to ask whether or not it may harm individuals, but is obliged to act with the one thought of securing the victory of the revolution over the bourgeoisie, the Cheka is obliged to defend the revolution and conquer the enemy even if its sword does by chance sometimes fall upon the heads of the innocent.'

[30] *Proletarskaya Revolyutsiya* 9(56) (1926), pp. 81-97.
F. *Dzerzhinsky, sbornik statei*, p. 147.
Lenin later alleged that the L.S.R.s were hypocrites for protesting against the use of the death penalty by the Revolutionary Tribunals, for he claimed that they had not objected to the shootings by 'Dzerzhinsky's Committee'. (Lenin, *op. cit.*, Vol. 23, p. 124.) The allegation appears to be untrue. They had protested not only in the Eboli case, but, according to Latsis (*Proletarskaya Revolyutsiya*, 9(56)), they had always voted against sentences of shooting in the Cheka 'Troiki', and Zaks, an L.S.R. Chekist who joined the Bolshevik Party in November 1918, had been reprimanded by his Central Committee for voting for a shooting. Peters (*F. Dzerzhinsky, sbornik statei*, p. 150), stated that there had been 'sharp disagreement' in VeCheKa with the L.R.S.s about the use of the death penalty.
[31] *Leninsky Sbornik*, Vol. 18, p. 169.
[32] The fullest Bolshevik account of these events is in Vol. I, pp. 107-390 of *Krasnaya Kniga VeCheKa*, edited by P. Makintsian, Moscow, 1920; a more concise account is in Lenin, *op. cit.*, Vol. 23, pp. 554-6. Savinkov (2) account is in B. V. Savinkov, *Borba s bolshevikami* (Warsaw, 1920), pp. 24-36. An L.S.R. account of the party's 'rising' is in J. Steinberg, *Spiridonova* (London, 1935), pp. 207-17.
[33] Reported by Svoboda Rossii, June 9, 1918, quoted in Bunyan, *Intervention, Civil War and Communism in Russia* (Baltimore, 1936), p. 227; and by Novaya Zhizn, June 8, 1918, quoted in Melgunov, *Krasnii Terror v Rossii* (Berlin, 1924), pp. 106-7. According to Radek (*F. Dzerzhinsky, sbornik statei*, p. 186), Dzerzhinsky gave this interview only to the remaining bourgeois papers.

On September 2, ostensibly as an answer to the attempted assassination of Lenin and the murder of Uritsky, the head of the Petrograd Cheka, on August 30, VTsIK adopted a resolution[34] calling on 'workers and peasants to reply to the White Terror by mass Red Terror'. The next day Petrovsky, the Commissar of Internal Affairs, issued a circular[35] to all Soviets ordering their Chekas and Militia to 'shoot unconditionally all who are engaged in White Guard activity', and demanding 'not the least wavering, not the least indecision in the application of mass terror'. On September 5 the famous Decree[36] 'On the Red Terror' announced that: 'Sovnarcom, having heard the report of the Chairman of Ve Cheka on the activity of the Commission, finds that in the given situation the safeguarding of the rear by means of terror is a direct necessity. . . .' The Decree ordered that:

(a) The Cheka should be strengthened by sending to it the largest possible number of Party members.

(b) Class enemies should be isolated in concentration camps.

(c) Anyone in contact with counter-revolutionary organs should be shot, and

(d) The names of all those shot and the reasons for their execution should be published.

An instruction[37] from Ve Cheka on September 17 empowered all Chekas to pass and execute sentences in cases of counter-revolution and serious breach of duty without referring them to the Revolutionary Tribunals.

Such an instruction was probably superfluous. Already from the first moment of its existence the Cheka began to undermine the position of the Revolutionary Tribunals and their authority to dispense 'revolutionary justice'. Shklovsky, a member of Ve Cheka, wrote[38]: 'The experience of the Cheka plainly indicates the harmfulness of subordinating to any authority an agency discharging such important tasks as the Cheka has assumed. . . . If someone should object that there are revolutionary laws, our reply must be that the methods of the Cheka are those very revolutionary laws, for no one can prove that the Cheka is striking at anyone but the enemies of the proletariat.' The Tribunals, according to their reports of 1918,[39] were powerless

[34] Reported in *Pravda*, September 3, 1918.
[35] *Izvestiya*, September 4, 1918. The circular is reproduced in W. H. Chamberlin: *The Russian Revolution, 1917-21*, 2nd edition (New York, 1952), p. 66.
[36] *R.S.F.S.R. Laws* (1918), 65: 710.   [37] Kozhevnikov, *op. cit.*, p. 89.
[38] *Ezhenedelnik Cheka*, No. 3, quoted in Bunyan, *op. cit.*, p. 259.
[39] 'Materiali N.K. Yustitsii', *Vypusk* 5 (1918), p. 53.

to prevent the Cheka from seizing and executing persons whose cases they were in the process of considering, or from transferring others from prison to Cheka concentration camps. The Cheka was seldom concerned to give publicity to the cases it investigated, and apparently only when it was so concerned did it hand them over for trial by Tribunal.

• The Tribunals had been established about a fortnight before the Cheka by the 'Decree No. 1 on the Courts', which also abolished all the existing judicial institutions and set up People's Courts. They were to try cases of counter-revolution, profiteering and sabotage, while other crimes and civil cases were to be dealt with by People's Courts. For a short time (December 1917 to March 1918) the Tribunals were under the control of the L.S.R. Steinberg. After his departure they were reorganized so as to consist of three members, one of whom came from the local Cheka. A Supreme Tribunal was attached to VTsIK and Tribunals were set up in the large towns. There was no right of appeal and the presence of the accused depended on the Tribunal's decision. The People's Courts were more slowly organized, and much of their work, to begin with, was done by the Tribunals. They maintained offices in the local Chekas ('Kameri narodnogo suda pri Che Ka') presumably because the Cheka found itself occasionally able to unload on to them some of the many minor, non-political, cases which it investigated.[40]

There were many attempts to hand back to the Tribunals some of the judicial powers which the Cheka had assumed from the first days of the Terror. None of these attempts had any lasting effect. The Cheka set up its own three-man courts or 'Troiki', which in April 1918 were reported to have delivered sentences on 400 anarchists in Moscow. At one period Ve Cheka had a 'Special Revolutionary Tribunal' attached to it for dealing with speculators and officials who committed breach of duty. It was decreed[41] that this Tribunal be 'guided in its judgments only by revolutionary interests, and not bound by any forms of legal procedure'. It was sometimes presided over by Dzerzhinsky. Even the ordinary Revolutionary Tribunals were liable to have Chekists as their president (Peters was for a time president of the Moscow Tribunal, and Latsis of the Military Tribunal of the Fifth Army.) The Cheka worked in co-operation with, or was directly represented on, a number of

[40] The 'Kameri' were set up in June 1921 (*R.S.F.S.R. Laws* (1921), 51: 294). See also *Entsiklopediya Gosudarstva i Prava*, Vol. 2, p. 1245.

[41] *R.S.F.S.R. Laws* (1919), 53: 504. Kozhevnikov, *op. cit.*, p. 90.

other Tribunals and semi-judicial organs which at one time or another were empowered to impose the death penalty. Military Tribunals, Field Court Martials and Commissions for combating desertion seem to have worked with the Cheka's 'special departments' in the armed forces. Railway Tribunals worked with the Cheka's transport departments. At the beginning of 1920 the Cheka's internal security troops ('Vokhr') set up a new system of Military Tribunals.[42] In May 1920 the Cheka was officially given the same powers as Revolutionary Tribunals when dealing with any crime 'directed against the security of the State'.[43] As late as June 1921 its powers to carry out 'extra-legal repression' in areas under martial law were confirmed.[44] In March 1920 the Cheka was permitted to despatch persons to forced labour camps by administrative decision for up to five years, if their investigations did not 'reveal sufficient evidence' for the Tribunals to start judicial proceedings.[45]

It is impossible to gauge with any accuracy the number of victims of the Cheka's terror. The figures of Cheka shootings and imprisonings given by Latsis[46] are obviously far too small. He did not even bother to add them up correctly, and they are contradicted by other official figures. The figures produced by the Whites are even more obviously far too large. According to Denikin,[47] 'the Special Judiciary Commission of Inquiry into the Bolshevik atrocities' reckoned the number of victims of the Bolshevist terror in 1918-19 at 1,700,000. 'But', admitted Denikin, 'their actual number is known to God alone.' Though the terror appears to have got into its stride only during the autumn of 1918, the United States Consul in Moscow reported back[48] on September 3 that 'since May' the Cheka had 'conducted an openly avowed campaign of terror', and that 'thousands of persons' had been 'summarily shot without even the form of trial'. The Petrograd papers had in fact the same day reported the execution of over 500 hostages for the murder of Uritsky, while at least 417 persons were reported to have been shot in connection with the Yaroslavl rising in June. The savagery increased as the civil war went on, and the Cheka was its chief agent on the Bolshevik side. Latsis already in August had announced[49] that there were no laws in civil war except one, according to which enemy wounded should be shot and no

[42] Kozhevnikov, *op. cit.*, p. 95.   [43] *R.S.F.S.R. Laws* (1920), 78: 370, 89: 454.
[44] *R.S.F.S.R. Laws* (1921), 51: 294.   [45] *R.S.F.S.R. Laws* (1920), 22, 23: 115.
[46] Latsis, *Dva goda borby na vnutrennom fronte* (Moscow, 1920), p. 75.
[47] Denikin: *The White Army* (London, 1930), p. 292.
[48] *Foreign Relations of the United States*, 1918, Vol. II (Washington, 1932), p. 387.
[49] *Izvestiya*, August 23, 1918.

prisoners should be taken. Countless victims fell to the special Cheka troops ('Vokhr' or 'Vnus') which carried out punitive expeditions and raids throughout the war, and also assisted in suppressing the Kronstadt rebellion, and, later, the Antonov peasant rising in Tambov.[50] W. H. Chamberlin gave[51] as his 'probably moderate estimate' the figure of 50,000 for those shot by the Cheka during the civil war.

According to all accounts the Tribunals had a far smaller share than the Cheka in the terror, yet the available evidence (which is probably more reliable than that concerning the Cheka) concerning their activity is impressive. Even after the end of the Civil War, during the first half of 1921, the Tribunals are stated[52] to have been passing death sentences at the rate of over 100 a month, and prison sentences at the rate of nearly 1,600 a month. Nearly 150,000 arrests were made by the organs of the Commissariat of Justice (i.e. by the Tribunals and the People's Courts) in the first half of 1919. The prisons of the Commissariat in February 1919 held 22,000 persons, 16,794 of whom still had their cases under investigation. Nearly half of these cases were being investigated by the Cheka, and the rest by the Tribunals or People's Courts.[53]

The end of the Civil War placed new responsibilities on the Cheka, particularly in the economic sphere. It is uncertain when the 'Economic Administration' of VeCheKa was first established, but, according to Latsis, it was one of the three main departments of the Central Cheka in 1921 and was responsible for 'combating counter-revolution in the economy'. Inter-departmental commissions consisting of representatives from important economic Commissariats and other organs were attached to VeCheKa to co-ordinate the battle against 'contrabanding and profiteering'.[54] When the granting of concessions to foreign countries for the development of economic resources was discussed at the Eighth Congress of Soviets in December 1920, a delegate proposed[55] that these operations should be controlled, on the political side by the Cheka and the Party, and on the economic side by the Cheka and Rabkrin. The Cheka would no doubt have been permitted to assume

[50] The Antonov movement was finally suppressed by the Red Army under Tukhachevsky (who also dealt with the Kronstadt rebels). At certain moments Antonov had 'several tens of thousands of men' under his command. (*Sovietskaya Voyennaya Entsiklopediya*, Vol. I, 1932, p. 566.)

[51] Chamberlin, *op. cit.*, Vol. 2, pp. 74-5.

[52] *N.K. Yustitsii, otchet IX omu Vserossiiskomu s'ezdu Sovetov* (1921), p. 23.

[53] *Sovetskaya Yustitsiya*, edited by Kursky (1919), p. 22.

[54] *R.S.F.S.R. Laws* (1919), 53: 504. (1921), 79: 674.

[55] *VIII S'ezd Sovetov, ezhenedelnyi byulleten S'ezda*, No. 5, December 25, 1920.

these responsibilities if anything had come of the concessions at this time. Though Lenin eventually proclaimed the necessity of restricting its activities to the political sphere, a Party resolution[56] only a few months earlier had called for the Cheka's assistance to control economic life under the N.E.P. regulations and to organize a new export trade.

The terror which the Cheka had practised during the Civil War, in order 'to defend the revolution and conquer the enemy', was scarcely modified by the arrival of peace. As it became more difficult to know whether it was striking friend or foe, the Cheka appears to have cared less, and to have relied on sentencing suspect groups to death or imprisonment *en bloc* for imaginary crimes of which the Cheka 'investigators' conceived them to be capable.[57] Many of the techniques developed by the Okhrana for the purpose of keeping the population under surveillance were adopted, but appear to have been employed with far less discrimination. The direction of this activity lay in the 'secret-political department', evidently the kernel of VeCheKa, which surveilled both civilian life and (through the 'special departments') the army. That the suppression of religious organizations was also a task in which the department interested itself, is suggested by the fact that the 'Troiki' established in the 'Guberniya' Soviets, to enforce the Decree (of January 23, 1918) on the separation of the Church from the State, consisted of a Chekist and two local officials.[58]

One of the hardest things to establish about the development of the Cheka is the real nature and strength of the opposition it aroused from Bolsheviks as well as non-Bolsheviks, and how smoothly the imposition of the police system was effected. The first active opposition came from Steinberg, the L.S.R. Commissar of Justice in the coalition Sovnarcom which the L.S.R.s entered on December 23, 1917, and left on March 15, 1918. Steinberg used his position to countermand Cheka instructions and attempt to impose legal restrictions on its activities. But these moves were speedily checked by the Bolshevik majority in Sovnarcom. The role of the L.S.R.s in the Cheka itself is more ambiguous.[59] The L.S.R. policy with regard to the Cheka, as

[56] 'Spravochnik partiinogo rabotnika', *Vypusk* 2 (1922), p. 178. Lenin, Vol. 29, p. 402. (A representative of VeCheKa was included on a Special Commission for Export attached to the Council of Labour and Defence on August 10, 1921.)
[57] An authentic, if rather tedious, account of the methods adopted by Cheka investigators may be found in R. V. Ivanov-Razumnik, *Tyurmi i Ssilki* (New York, 1953).
[58] *N.K. Yustitsii, otchet . . .* , p. 42.
[59] The Bolshevik account of Steinberg's opposition is in *Leninsky Sbornik*, Vol. 21 (1933), pp. 110-17. Steinberg's account is in J. Steinberg, *Souvenirs d'un Commissaire*

explained by Steinberg, was to try to transform it into a 'technical service' at the disposal of the organs of justice and thus to avert the Bolshevik terror, from which the L.S.R.s, he claimed, totally disassociated themselves (notably in their leader Spiridonova's open letter[60] to the Bolsheviks of November 1918, which contrasted the 'classical', social revolutionary conception of terror with that of the Bolshevik Party). It was with this aim in view that the Party sought admission to the Cheka and, after overcoming strong opposition from Lenin, were given places in it. Though this account is more convincing than the Bolshevik one, according to which the L.S.R.s were invited to participate in the Cheka by Dzerzhinsky as personal friends and immediately betrayed his trust by undermining its work in order to discredit the Bolsheviks, it is doubtful whether the L.S.R.s ever had an effective policy at all. Their participation in the Cheka was as much a political blunder as their murder of Mirbach and their miniature protest 'rising' in July which led to their being outlawed.

On the occasions on which they were permitted to express their criticism of the regime, the other non-Bolshevik Socialist parties continued to denounce the Cheka. At the Seventh Congress of Soviets in December 1919, Martov protested at the Cheka's 'monstrous growth' (by 1921 it numbered, according to Latsis, 31,000,[61] whereas the N.K.V.D., an important Commissariat even then, reported that it numbered only 2,823).[62] At the Eighth Congress in December 1920, Dan accused it of giving orders to VTsIK about the persons to whom amnesties should be granted. On both these occasions Lenin ridiculed the charges and the Mensheviks who had formulated them. Prominent among the accusations brought against the Bolsheviks by the Kronstadt insurgents of March 1921 was that of having 'brought the workers, instead of freedom, an ever present fear of being dragged into the torture chambers of the Cheka, which exceeds by many times in its horrors the gendarmerie administration of the Tsarist regime.'[63]

The protests of foreigners against the Cheka's terror only provided opportunities for Bolshevik propagandists to practise their skill in polemical writing. Chicherin set a high standard

du peuple, 1917-18 (Paris, 1930). See also Decrees issued by Steinberg: *R.S.F.S.R. Laws* (1917), 9: 145 (on the power of arrest), and 9: 146 (on prison regulations).

[60] The letter is reproduced in Steinberg, *Spiridonova*, pp. 236-7.
[61] Latsis, *Chrezvychainye Komissii . . .* , p. 12.
[62] *Otchet o deyatelnosti N.K.V.D. za pervoe polugodie 1921* (1921), p. 10.
[63] *Izvestiya Vremennogo Revolyutsionnogo Komiteta Matrosov, Krasnoarmeitsev i Rabochikh goroda Kronshtata*, March 8, 1921, No. 6.

in September 1918 in his replies to the protest delivered on behalf of the Diplomatic Corps in Moscow by the Swiss Minister and to another by the head of the American Red Cross.[64] Trotsky found his best form in his *Defence of Terrorism* (1921) directed against Kautsky. Lenin took the offensive with his refrain[65]: 'The Entente thrust the Terror upon us.' After the Civil War a greater sensitiveness to foreign opinion about the Cheka seems to have developed, and with it the process of attempting to deceive selected foreigners (such as the British Labour Delegations to Russia) who enquired about it.

There was, however, a good deal of internal resistance to the Cheka which could not immediately be discredited as counter-revolutionary. When the central Cheka first enlisted the help of the local Soviets, in March 1918, in setting up local Chekas, the plan seems to have been that the Soviets were to retain a measure of control over them. This was at any rate the view of the N.K.V.D., which was the co-ordinating Commissariat in charge of the Soviets, and which through them already controlled the Militia. An N.K.V.D. instruction to the local Soviets in June 1918, signed by Latsis (who, before becoming a Chekist, began his career in the N.K.V.D.) requested them to organize an administrative department ('Otdel upravleniya') consisting of three sub-departments ('Podotdeli'): Information, Militia and Cheka.[66] But the subordination of the Chekas to the local Soviets was never effected. Relations between them became very strained when both the N.K.V.D. and VeCheKa sent conflicting instructions to the local Soviets, and when the heads of local Chekas and Soviets attempted to arrest each other.[67] At the first conference of representatives of 'Guberniya' Soviets in August 1918 a resolution was passed which formally demanded that the local Chekas be reduced to the status of sub-departments of the Soviets. VeCheKa immediately denounced the resolution and issued instructions to the Chekas to maintain their 'autonomy'.[68]

On October 18 *Pravda* published an article by Dukhovsky, Secretary of the N.K.V.D. collegium, in which he asserted that

---

[64] *Foreign Relations of the United States* (1918), Vol. II, pp. 685-6, 697-8, 705-8, 714-15.

[65] Lenin, *op. cit.*, Vol. 24, p. 402 (broadcast replies to an American journalist, July 1919), p. 425 (speech to a meeting of education workers, August 1919), p. 567 (speech to a Party Conference, December 1919), and p. 604 (speech at Seventh Congress of Soviets, December 1919).

[66] *Vestnik N.K.V.D.*, Nos. 15, 16 (June 1918), p. 2.

[67] A good eye-witness account of such mutual arrests in the Tver district is in *Arkhiv Russkoi Revolyutsii* (Berlin, 1923), Vol. 8, pp. 80-81.

[68] *Izvestiya*, October 20, 1918. Latsis, *Chrezvychainye Komissii . . .*, p. 57-8.

the relations between the Chekas and the Soviets was one of the most burning questions of the day. The struggle for power between them was sometimes being urged under the slogan, 'All power to the Chekas!' This slogan would replace 'All power to the Soviets!' if the Chekas were not effectively subordinated to the Soviets. *Izvestiya* on October 17, in view of 'the recent press campaign against the activity of the Cheka, and the suggestion that it should be subordinated to a Commissariat', interviewed the Chekist, Peters. Peters was reported as saying: 'In vain do many naive comrades think that the time has come to limit the Cheka's activities. . . . All this noise and lamentation about the energetic and firm measures of the Cheka does not deserve the attention it is given; it could only come from comrades who are occupied in journalism in offices and not in actively fighting the enemies of the proletariat.' This provoked an indignant reply from Olminsky,[69] who remarked that Lenin himself had spent a lot of time occupied in journalism in offices which had not been unprofitable for the proletariat; and from Tikhomirov, in *Izvestiya*,[70] on behalf of the N.K.V.D. The N.K.V.D. it appeared, had sent a circular round the local Soviets requesting their views on relations with the Chekas. Out of 147 replies to this circular, 118 had favoured the subordination of the Chekas to the Soviets. But the opinion of the Soviets, no matter its degree of unanimity, counted little in the councils of the Bolshevik Party, and when the Cheka's powers were 'discussed' by VTsIK in the autumn of 1918 (unfortunately no record of the proceedings appears to be available), the only result was the 'Statutes' of the Cheka, which provided that it should do no more than 'work in close contact with the N.K.V.D.' Friction between the two organs continued for a while, but must finally have subsided after the appointment of Dzerzhinsky in 1920 as head of the N.K.V.D. as well as the Cheka.

Perhaps the most serious threat to the consolidation of the Cheka came from those who wished to see its functions performed by the Revolutionary Tribunals. The Commissar of Justice, Kursky, alleged[71] that 'the wide distribution of Chekas throughout every "Uyezd" of Soviet Russia at the end of 1918 created a natural reaction against the lawless character of their activity, and this was expressed in a quite violent controversy, in the press and at Party meetings, between the partisans of the Tribunals and those of the Cheka.'

[69] *Pravda*, October 26, 1918.   [70] *Izvestiya*, October 20, 1918.
[71] *Sovetskaya Yustitsiya*, edited by Kursky, pp. 11-13.

The foremost representative of this opposition to the Cheka was Krylenko, who, though his post was that of Chief Prosecutor of the Supreme Tribunal, carried more weight than the Commissar of Justice. Both Latsis and Peters refer (without adverse comment, for Krylenko's reputation was unassailable till the purges of the late thirties) to Krylenko as a persistent critic of the Cheka. It was apparently[72] he who brought about the discussion on the Cheka's powers in VTsIK, and who, according to an American journalist,[73] became known in Moscow as the man who had 'curbed the powers of the Cheka'. His wife, Razmirovitch, also a prominent figure in the Tribunals, is said by Steinberg to have been of assistance in Steinberg's own brief campaign against the Cheka. What is known about Krylenko suggests that he did not oppose the Cheka on account of its 'lawlessness' (though this may have been Kursky's motive) but because he was jealous of a rival system.

Presumably as a result of pressure from Krylenko, numerous Decrees were passed during 1918-21 defining and re-defining the division of responsibility between the Tribunals and the Cheka; but whatever ground the Tribunals gained during the less bloodthirsty periods of the intervention and civil war the Cheka more than made up in times of crisis. Even the transformation of the Cheka into the G.P.U. in 1923, represented at the time as a triumph for the principle of 'revolutionary legality', did nothing to strengthen the position of the courts *vis à vis* the police; and Vyshinsky was bold enough to advance the opinion that the difference between the courts and the O.G.P.U. 'followed the same line' as that which had existed between the Tribunals and the Cheka.[74]

The Tribunals made most headway against the Cheka early in 1919. In January the 'Uyezd' Chekas were abolished; and this, according to Moroz, had been taken by 'some comrades' as a victory in the campaign against the Cheka.[75] (Such comrades must have been disillusioned when it was revealed that these Chekas had not been abolished at all, but simply disguised as 'political departments' in the 'Uyezd' Militia.[76]) In February a Decree[77] was passed, according to which, 'The power of pronouncing sentences in all cases arising in the Chekas is handed over to reorganized Tribunals.' The Tribunals were also permitted to check investigations by the Cheka and

[72] *Arkhiv Russkoi Revolyutsii*, Vol. 8, p. 71.
[73] F. A. Mackenzie, *Russia before dawn* (London, 1923), p. 36.
[74] Vyshinsky and Undrevich, *Kurs ugolovnogo protsessa* (1936), p. 202.
[75] *Pravda*, January 31, 1919.　　　[76] Latsis, *Chrezvychainye Komissii . . .*, p. 28.
[77] *R.S.F.S.R. Laws* (1919), 12: 130.

to inspect its prisons and free those who had been illegally confined in them. 'Direct punishments' were henceforward to be administered by the Cheka only in areas under martial law. Only a few months later Kursky sorrowfully admitted[78] that it had not been possible to implement 'the humane principles' of this Decree, due to 'the realities of the savage Civil War'. But Krylenko was able to celebrate at least one genuine triumph over the Cheka, and over Dzerzhinsky personally, at the trial in the middle of February by the Supreme Revolutionary Tribunal of the Chekist Kosarev.[79]

Kosarev, according to the report of the trial, had been sentenced to ten years 'katorga' in 1908 for murder and robbery. After the revolution he had secured his release by pretending he had been a 'political', and obtained a job with VeCheKa. In September 1918 Dzerzhinsky had personally appointed him Assistant Chairman of VeCheKa's Control and Inspection Commission, which received and investigated all complaints about illegal actions by Chekists and Soviet officials. He was now on trial, charged with having used his position to extort large sums of money, which had enabled him to lead a luxurious life—according to his own confession he had accumulated 100,000 roubles in the International Bank of Chicago. It appeared that Chekists such as Kosarev were in the habit of accepting bribes from the relatives of persons held under investigation, to transfer cases to the Tribunals. Dzerzhinsky attended the trial in support of Kosarev. He objected to details about the Cheka's work being made public, and characterized Kosarev as 'an experienced and conscientious investigator', denying any knowledge of his criminal past, and hoped he would 'not be sacrificed in the struggle of political passions which has centred round the Cheka'. Krylenko, who appeared as prosecutor (and had probably managed the trial from the start), denied the accusation, in Dzerzhinsky's last remark, that he was more interested in discrediting the Cheka than in Kosarev's innocence or guilt; and demanded that Kosarev be shot and the Cheka purged of all such Chekists, 'who disgraced the revolution'. Kosarev's defence vainly cited the absence of any Decree authorizing the use of the death penalty; he was sentenced to be shot. Not the least part of Krylenko's triumph must have been that *Pravda* carried full reports of the trial which ran over four days.

[78] *Sovetskaya Yustitsiya*, edited by Kursky, pp. 11-13.
[79] Reported in *Pravda*, February 14-18, 1919. The case is also referred to in Melgunov, *op. cit.*, pp. 182-3.

But Krylenko's victory in the Kosarev case and in other less important ones, reported about the same time,[80] in which Chekists were successfully prosecuted by Tribunals, was small compensation for his failure to appropriate, for any length of time, for the Tribunals any of the Cheka's powers. This failure appears to have rankled long after, judging by the tendentious account of relations between the Tribunals and the Cheka which Krylenko contributed to the Encyclopaedia of State and Law[81] (published under Stuchka's editorship in 1925-7). The account based the Tribunals' claim to perform the Cheka's functions not on any necessity to impose legal restrictions on the terror—there is no suggestion of this—but simply on the alleged fact that these functions had originally been assigned to them and not to the Cheka, which had merely taken advantage of certain regrettable weaknesses in the initial structure of the Tribunals to substitute itself for them as the instrument of the terror.

Krylenko's story, and particularly his explanation of how the Tribunals came to 'yield' their role to the Cheka, is not convincing. He confuses rather than strengthens it by the unusual assertion that the Cheka was founded (for what purpose he does not say) 'long before' the Tribunals, by a Decree of November 2 (November 15, New Style), and that the original text of the 'Decree No. 1 on the Courts' had defined the Tribunals as 'organs for combating counter-revolution'.[82] Perhaps all that can be learned from his account is the extent to which, even in the early years of the regime, the facts of Soviet history were at the mercy of Bolshevik personalities who desired to give it a particular slant.[83]

[80] *Pravda* on December 4, 1918, reported the trial of another Chekist, Vartapetov, and, on February 20, 1919, the trial of the heads of the Volokolamsk Cheka.

[81] *Entsiklopediya Gosudarstva i prava*, Vol. 3, pp. 683-90.

[82] There is no trace of any such Decree of November 2 concerning the Cheka. (However, Krylenko may conceivably have had in mind some decision of that date regarding the security department of the Petrograd Military-Revolutionary Committee.) The original text of the Decree No. 1 on the courts is available in 'Materiali N.K. Yustitsii', *Vypusk* 2 (1918), p. 104. It does not even mention the Revolutionary Tribunals far less define them as 'organs for fighting counter-revolution'. But there may have been yet another draft of the text incorporating Krylenko's views on the Tribunals. Stuchka, who seems to have shared Krylenko's ambitions for the Tribunals, wrote in *Pravda* in January 1918 that, 'according to the meaning of the Decree', they were not courts but organs for fighting counter-revolution. ('Materiali N.K. Yustitsii', *Vypusk* 2, 1918, pp. 11-15.)

[83] Krylenko gave much the same account of relations between the Tribunals and the Cheka in *Sudoustroistvo v R.S.F.S.R.*, 1923. These views on the subject were not finally branded as unorthodox until Vyshinsky, in the late thirties, began his campaign to discredit him. (Vyshinsky and Undrevich: *Kurs ugolovnogo protsessa*, 1936, p. 202.)

Not only did the Cheka have to reckon with the opposition of other governmental bodies, which, like the Tribunals or the N.K.V.D. directly blocked the way to its expansion, or which, like the army and the economic Commissariats, resented its incursions into their fields of operation and the arbitrary arrests which deprived them of their personnel; it also could not at first afford to neglect popular feeling.

The Cheka's difficulty lay in the fact that, from the outset, it was obvious that it met the hostility of the very proletariat on whose behalf is was supposedly wielding the terror. Moroz described[84] how during 1918, 'the Chekas came to be considered as something superfluous and even harmful to our revolution. Matters went so far that Chekists were called "inquisitors" and "okhranists". The Chekas themselves were called "torture chambers", "Bastilles", etc.' 'An atmosphere was created', confessed Latsis,[85] 'which killed any desire to work in this necessary organ of state power.' It is uncertain to what extent this abhorence of the Cheka may have been shared by some members of the Bolshevik Party. But at the end of 1918, during the short period when the Cheka was subjected to 'criticism and self-criticism', it came under the fire of a prominent Bolshevik journalist, Olminsky.[86] Olminsky was permitted to write in *Pravda*[87] that there were differences of opinion in the Party, whether and how far the arrests and executions carried out by the Cheka were really necessary, and that he was 'appalled' that under the existing Cheka regulations the local Chekas could shoot nearly any Party member they wished. In another *Pravda*[88] article he protested at the 'scandalous' and 'inhuman' behaviour of a local Cheka at Nikolsk which had stripped and flogged a number of peasants.

Latsis and Peters made a clumsy attempt to explain away the hostility to the Cheka by arguing that its purpose had been misunderstood by the proletariat, who had naively failed to distinguish between its methods and those of their old oppressor, the Okhrana. They further asserted that while the proletariat had boycotted the Cheka, criminals in disguise had managed to slip into its service and 'made use of the title of Chekist agent to blackmail, extort, and fill their pockets'. It was these criminals, and not genuine Chekists, who were responsible for the worst outrages. For good measure, Latsis also suggested

---

[84] *Pravda*, January 21, 1919.   [85] Latsis, *Chrezvychainye Komissii* . . . , p. 10.
[86] Olminsky had joined the staff of *Vpered* in 1905. He was eventually put in charge of the Party History Committee ('Istpart'), attached to the Central Committee, and became a director of the Marx-Engels Institute.
[87] *Pravda*, October 8, 1918.   [88] *Pravda*, December 19, 1918.

that even genuine Chekists might be forgiven an occasional lapse, for: 'No matter how honest and crystal clear a man may be, the work of the Cheka, which is carried out with almost unrestricted powers and in circumstances which are exceptionally trying for his nerves, will tell upon him. Only in rare cases do Chekists remain unaffected by these conditions of work.'[89] These arguments can have deceived no one, particularly after Dzerzhinsky's defence of the criminal Chekist, Kosarev, and after a report by a local Cheka had announced that it had recruited an ex-Okhrana officer as an agent.[90] (Recruiting of senior Chekists seems to have been carried out at first by Dzerzhinsky on a personal basis; later it was increasingly staffed by Party members of several years standing,[91] and they were posted to and from the Cheka by the Orgbureau of the Central Committee, established in March 1919 and dominated by Stalin.[92] Recruiting of agents and informers was left to the discretion of the local Chekas.)

By the end of 1918 it was necessary for Lenin to come to the support of the Cheka and he did so by accusing its critics of insufficient Marxism. The report of his speech shows it to have been an uninspired performance: '. . . naturally the mistakes of the Cheka attract attention most of all. A narrow-minded intelligentsia is seizing on these mistakes without wishing to go further to the root of the matter. What surprises me about the howls over the Cheka's mistakes is the inability to take a large view of the question. We have people who seize on particular mistakes by the Cheka, sob and fuss over them. . . . The trouble, of course, lies not in the Cheka personnel, but in the nature of their activity, which requires decisiveness, speed and, above all, trustworthiness. When I consider the Cheka's activity and compare it with these attacks, I say: this is narrow-minded, idle talk which is worthless. . . . Marx said: between capitalism

[89] Latsis, *Chrezvychrinye Komissii*, p. 11. Very much the same argument could still be used to justify the police ten years later. Peters wrote: 'In the work of VeCheKa and the G.P.U. there were and are many temptations. . . . No one has to come in closer contact with dying bourgeois society than do the members of VeCheKa or G.P.U.' Bukharin, whose tributes to the police were particularly extravagant (see, e.g., his article on its tenth anniversary in *Pravda*, December 18, 1927), put it as follows: 'Do not let us forget how many of those (Chekists) who remain are nervous wrecks, and sometimes hopelessly ill. For their work was such torture, it demanded such gigantic concentration, it was such hellish work, that a truly iron character was required.' (*F. E. Dzerzhinsky Sbornik Statei*, 1931, pp. 143, 158.)　　[90] *Ezhenedelnik Cheka*, No. 5, quoted in Bunyan, p. 247.

[91] A special commission of the Council of Labour and Defence on December 3, 1918 decided that responsible Cheka posts should be held only by Party members of at least two years standing. (*Leninsky Sbornik*, Vol. 21, p. 226.)

[92] 'Spravochnik partiinogo rabotnika', *Vypusk* 2 (1922), p. 178, contains an Orgburo instruction posting Party members to the Cheka.

and communism lies the revolutionary dictatorship of the proletariat. The more the proletariat crushes the bourgeoisie the more furiously will it strike back. . . . When we are reproached with cruelty, we wonder how people can forget the most elementary Marxism. . . . It is quite understandable that alien elements should attach themselves to the Cheka. We will knock them off by self-criticism. The important thing for us is that the Chekas are directly carrying out the dictatorship of the proletariat, and in this respect their role is invaluable. . . .'[93]

At about the same time Lenin publicly corrected one of the chief exponents of the terror, Latsis, whom he was nevertheless careful to describe as 'one of the best, experienced communists', for pushing 'elementary Marxism' too far in the terror. Latsis had urged his subordinates not to seek for evidence that their prisoners had opposed the Soviets, but to settle their fate on the basis of their class, origin, education and occupation, for this was 'the meaning and essence of the Red Terror'. Lenin announced that this was 'rubbish', and that what Latsis had really wished to say was only that: 'the Red Terror is a forcible suppression of the exploiters who attempt to restore their power.'[94]

In this way Lenin apparently hoped to bring to heel both 'rightist' and 'leftist' deviators on the subject of the Terror, without making clear how the Marxism which he quoted at them guided the work of the Cheka in practice, or whom precisely the Terror was directed against.

It was necessary to keep the connection between Marxism and the Cheka vague, in order to represent the latter's function as the waging of war against counter-revolutionaries according to Marxist principles, when in reality it was concerned with holding together the Bolshevist regime by the indiscriminate application of force whenever and wherever expedient. The further extension of the Cheka's activities after the end of the Civil War was accounted for by another fiction: the necessity for the Cheka to carry on its fight on a broader front against counter-revolutionaries who had only been forced underground, not annihilated, and had infiltrated and disguised their forces throughout the state apparatus. Latsis wrote in 1921[95]: 'In all spheres of our life the counter-revolution has developed. It is

[93] *Pravda*, December 18, 1918, reproduced in Lenin, *op. cit.*, Vol. 23, p. 272.
[94] Latsis' article appeared in *Pravda*, December 25, 1918, and in *Krasnyi Terror*, No. 1, November 1918. It is reproduced in Bunyan, p. 261. Lenin's criticism of the article is in Vol, 23. p. 458 ('A little picture for explaining big questions'). Latsis was also severely criticized by Yaroslavsky in *Pravda*, December 29, 1918.
[95] Latsis, *Chrezvychainye Komissii . . .*, p. 24.

therefore obvious that the work of VeCheKa must cover all spheres of Soviet life where counter-revolution has roots. And this means that there is no sphere of life not covered by the activity of VeCheKa. It must watch everything: military life, food, education, positively all economic organs, health, outbreaks of fire, communications, etc.'

But by the end of 1921, Lenin found it necessary to attempt a more ambitious deception concerning the police. He told the Ninth Congress of Soviets: 'Our failings are sometimes continuations of our virtues. This is the case with VeCheKa. It was virtuous when it defended the revolution against countless foreign enemies, when it was our striking weapon against countless plots. . . . But now, under present circumstances, it is imperative to restrict this institution to the purely political sphere. We say definitely that it is necessary to reform VeCheKa.' The Congress duly noted 'the heroic work of VeCheKa in the Civil War', and considered that the strengthening of Soviet authority, both internal and external, permitted the sphere of VeCheKa's activities to be narrowed down, and judicial organs to be made responsible for carrying out the fight against infractions of the law. In February 1922 the Cheka was replaced by the G.P.U. Events quickly demonstrated that nothing concerning the police except its name had been changed, but the myth of its constitutional respectability was now firmly emplanted in Soviet propaganda.

SIBERIAN PARTISANS IN THE CIVIL WAR

By David Footman

(i)

LENIN, at the All-Russian Congress of Soviets on December 5, 1919, remarked that 'Kolchak had occasioned a vast series of risings in Siberia, on which we are receiving exact reports from our comrades; and which are ensuring for us a complete recovery, this time a conscious and deliberate recovery, of Siberia.'[1] This statement, as the following pages will attempt to show, must be taken with some reserve. It is true that the Partisan movement made an important contribution to the defeat of the White cause. It is true that the considerable areas occupied at various times for various periods by various Partisan groups were ruled, for the most part, under some sort of Soviet system. But perhaps the most interesting feature of the Partisan movement in Siberia is its degree of spontaneity and independence of outside influence. One of the few outstanding Partisan leaders who was also a member of the Bolshevik Party has recorded: 'The difficulty of the struggle was increased in that for the whole period . . . there was no contact whatsoever with any urban organization, and therefore the movement was left exclusively to our own efforts.'[2] The movement was entirely a peasant one, and politics had never taken deep root in Siberian villages. As a White historian has rightly remarked of Bolshevik-Socialist Revolutionary rivalries, 'the replacement of one kind of socialism by another was a kind of parlour game, incomprehensible to the sturdy peasant mind.'[3] The basis of the Partisan movement was the peasant's reaction to attempts by the authorities in the towns to interfere with him. The form of organization, military and civil, that the movement took was the one that came naturally to the peasant when and if left to organize himself. And by this very fact it became a problem to the Soviet leadership as soon as the Civil War was over.

[1] Lenin, *Sochinenie*, Vol. XXIV, p. 599, quoted in *Za Vlast Sovietov* (Novosibirsk 1947), p. 20.
[2] V. G. Yakovenko, *Zapiski Partizana* (Moscow-Leningrad, 1925), p. 104.
[3] G. K. Gins, *Sibir, Soiuzniki i Kolchak* (Pekin 1921), Vol. I, p. 48.

(ii)

The documentation of the Partisan movement is a matter of some difficulty. Partisan headquarters, by their very nature, do not amass full records. Of the records that existed, much was destroyed in the course of the Civil War. What survives is in the keeping of various Party institutions in Moscow, Novosibirsk and elsewhere, who show great selectivity in the matter of release. Such accounts by participants as were published in the twenties are now out of print and difficult to locate. But the historian's major handicap, as in other fields, is in the twists and turns of the official Party line. In the earlier volumes of the (old) Large Soviet Encyclopaedia the only Siberian Partisan to be mentioned by name is the Bolshevik Yakovenko.[4] The volume containing the article on the Partisan movement came out eight years later.[5] It features quotations from Lenin on Partisan shortcomings and limitations, and gives no name of any Siberian leader. It is true that favourable mention is made of Chapaev and Lazo who operated in the Urals and the Far East respectively; but as both were dead by the spring of 1920 they had had little chance to succumb to deviation. It must be remembered that I. N. Smirnov and his main associates in the Revolutionary Military Soviet of the Fifth Red Army (who recovered Siberia for the Bolsheviks) were victims of the purges of the thirties. And so the collection *Za Vlast Sovietov* (Ogiz, Novosibirsk, 1947) suppresses all mention of Yakovenko, who perhaps of all Partisans had made the greatest personal contribution to the Red Army's victories; while Mamontov, Gromov and Kravchenko are brought out of oblivion and reinstated as heroes. The introduction to this work, by I. G. Zobachev, apparently seeks to ascribe the main credit for the inception of the movement to Stalin personally on the somewhat flimsy grounds that Sverdlov sent him a telegram on January 11, 1919, to ask what was being done about organizing underground activities from Perm.[6]

(iii)

The general pattern of the Partisan revolts is a simple one. The first two risings of any importance both took place in the autumn of 1918, before Kolchak's accession to power, in areas about 150 miles south of the Trans-Siberian railway. In September some thousands of peasants, called up for military

---

[4] Under Yakovenko in Vol. LXV issued 1931. (There is however the possibly ominous entry that he resigned from his functions in 1926 on the grounds of ill health.)   [5] Vol. XLVI (1939).   [6] *Za Vlast Sovietov*, p. 21.

service with the army, revolted and captured the town of Slavgorod to the south-west of Novonikolaevsk. A week or so later they were ejected and the revolt suppressed. Shortly afterwards, some 300 miles to the east, peasant bands were a serious threat to the town of Minusinsk until their defeat and liquidation at the hands of the government forces.

A few days after the proclamation of Kolchak as Supreme Ruler a small band, later commanded by Kravchenko, captured the village of Stepnoi-Badzhei, somewhat nearer the main railway line and south-south-east of Krasnoiarsk. A month later a larger band led by Shchetinkin occupied a few villages to the north of Achinsk. At the turn of the year Yakovenko with twenty followers captured Taseevo, 150 miles to the north of Kansk.

These three groups were, for the time being, the most important of Kolchak's Partisan opponents. Detachments were sent out from the nearest garrisons to suppress them. In each case the detachments were inadequate in numbers, organization and morale, and the expeditions failed. To the Partisans such victories meant more rifles and ammunition, more prestige, and more recruits and support from the surrounding villages. Accordingly, subsequent and stronger expeditions came up against immeasurably tougher opponents. However, by late March 1919 Shchetinkin's band found themselves hopelessly outnumbered and surrounded. They took the decision to break through. The operation was successful as was the subsequent trek in a long loop to the west and south; and after a month's hard marching and skirmishing they joined up with Kravchenko at Stepnoi-Badzhei. For the rest of the campaign the Kravchenko-Shchetinkin forces acted as a single army.

The next few weeks saw a comparative lull. In and round Taseevo and Stepnoi-Badzhei the Partisans were busy building up their military strength and organizing their territory. By this time the potential threat to the Trans-Siberian railway was fully recognized at Kolchak's headquarters; but the Czech and other allied contingents were now taking over guard duties along the line, and time was needed to prepare what was now realised must be a major operation. In late May and June the two-fold White offensive was launched, northwards and southwards. On both fronts Partisan resistance was overwhelmed. Taseevo and Stepnoi-Badzhei were both evacuated. Yakovenko retreated into the Northern taiga and along this front ensued a temporary stalemate. Kravchenko and Shchetinkin trekked southwards. They reached Uriankhai (now Tanu-Tuva) on the borders of Mongolia with the intention of crossing Mongolia to join up with Red forces in Turkestan. A small Cossack detachment sent after them was defeated near Belotsarsk (Kyzyl). By now however it was obvious that the tide of the Civil War in Siberia was flowing strongly in favour of the Reds. Kravchenko and Shchetinkin abandoned the idea of Turkestan, and turned north again. In September they reached Minusinsk and took the town against weak opposition.

Meanwhile, since March and April, Partisan groups had been operating in various parts of the Altai. In September these bands united under the supreme command of Mamontov and became, numerically, by far the largest of the Partisan armies. But the vastness of the area involved, and, in particular their distance from the all important artery of the Trans-Siberian railway, made them of lower priority in the eyes of the Omsk headquarters as compared with the Taseevo and Stepnoi-Badzhei groups: and the organization of a major offensive against them was not taken in hand until late autumn on the eve of the White collapse.

In late October the Fifth Red Army took Tobolsk and Petropavlovsk and the Kolchak regime started to disintegrate. Outlying garrisons were withdrawn for fear of being cut off. Whole units deserted *en masse*. In November and December the Partisan armies, 'growing like mushrooms'[7] with ever increasing swarms of new recruits, pressed on against the main centres, with little to oppose them beyond the severity of a Siberian winter. Mamontov's troops took Slavgorod, Kamen, Semipalatinsk and Barnaul. Kravchenko and Shchetinkin came northwards towards Achinsk and Krasnoiarsk; Yakovenko came south into Kansk. And further east were numerous smaller groups—among them 'Grandpa' Karandashvili and his five hundred horsemen—converging upon Irkutsk.

The Partisans' contribution to the Soviet recovery of Siberia is not to be measured in terms of casualties inflicted upon the Whites. Pitched battles were few and, as often as not, ended in Partisan defeats. Nor had the insurgents much success as saboteurs. A few trains were derailed by Kravchenko in the Achinsk area, and a few more by the Shitkino group of the Taseevo Partisans to the east of Kansk. But considering the length and vulnerability of the main railway it is remarkable how little traffic was help up. It is true that much manpower was tied down in guarding the line; but most of the troops concerned were Czechs and others who, by 1919, were useless

[7] Kantyshev, in *Proletarska Revoliutsia*, No. 22 (1923), p. 171.

for the purpose of fighting the Red Army at the front. Partisan contribution should rather be measured by what they denied to the Whites. All through the campaign the Kolchak forces were short of men, of horses and supplies. Of course these shortages were hugely accentuated by White incompetence: but once the Partisans got going there were large and increasing areas from which no men and no supplies could be obtained, and into which an ever increasing flow of recalcitrant peasants and unwilling recruits could fly for refuge. And above all there was the moral factor. The Partisan movements were a practical alternative to Omsk. They stood for freedom from injustice, from extortion and from interference. They seemed to satisfy that inarticulate longing for a peasant Utopia, which so many Siberian peasants came vaguely, temporarily and passionately to associate with a Soviet regime.

(iv)

Soviet writers of the twenties are at pains to ascribe the Siberian Partisan movement to the class structure of the Siberian peasantry and to emphasize the role of the newer immigrants, the Novoseli, and of the poorer peasants generally as against that of the Starozhili. These last were descendants of the old-timers who, being first in the field, had secured the best and most accessible land. Weaklings had died or left. Those that remained made good and handed on prosperous farms to their children. They had the conservatism of a class with something to lose. The Novoseli represented the mass immigration of more recent decades, who had to take what land they could get. Their holdings were smaller, poorer and less handy for markets. They were inadequately equipped. There was often not enough to support a family, and young men went off to find jobs on the railway or in mines or factories. Furthermore the Novoseli had recent memories of hardship at the hands of officials and land-lords in Russia. Theoretically they were the stuff to produce a revolution.

The following comparative table has been produced in support of this theory:

District	Proportion of Starozhili	Proportion of Novoseli
Achinsk	39%	61%
Kansk	23%	77%
Krasnoiarsk	50%	50%
Minusinsk	53%	47%
Yeniseisk	42%	58%[8]

[8] Maksakov and Turunov, *Partizanskoe Dvizhenie v Sibiri* (Moscow-Leningrad, 1925), p. 6.

But it is difficult for a non-Marxist to agree that these figures mean anything at all. The Minusinsk peasants, with their majority of Starozhili, fought the Whites at least as hard as any of the others. And even in the Kansk area, with its large majority of Novoseli, we have the authority of Yakovenko himself for stating that the backbone of the movement was the relatively well-to-do middle peasant—of whom a typical household of two or three adult males would possess a holding of twenty-four to thirty acres with six horses, eight cows or oxen and twenty sheep or pigs.[9]

Later Soviet writers naturally emphasize the role of the Party. 'The Central Committee of the Party, Lenin, Stalin, Sverdlov, assumed control of the Siberian underground organizations, guided their organizational work, made it possible to stir up the masses to the fight against the Kolchak regime.'[10]

The defeat of the Siberian Bolsheviks in the summer of 1918 by the Czechs and the various Russian anti-Bolshevik groups had been speedy and complete. However, surviving Party members did succeed within the next few weeks in building up an underground organization that remained in more or less effective existence for several months. The first Siberian Regional Underground Bolshevik Congress met in Tomsk in mid-August and decided on preparations for a general armed rising.[11] The second Congress, also at Tomsk, in late November went further into the question. Some delegates feared that local risings would only dissipate the Party's strength. Others held the risk of defeat to be preferable to the psychological consequences of inaction. It was finally decided that local risings should be considered as the first step towards a general rising.[12] Accordingly the Omsk Committee (where there were 600 Party members, and numerous sympathizers in the garrison) decided to act on December 22. The revolt went off at half cock and was suppressed with heavy losses to the Party.

In January the Soviet authorities in Russia set up a Ural-Siberian Buro, a Party organization based on Soviet territory and designed to direct underground work in Siberia by means of line crossers. A number of these couriers did arrive and did contact what was left of the Omsk Committee. They brought letters from Sverdlov and money, totalling nearly half a million roubles. But little of this could be distributed because of the

[9] Yakovenko, *Zapiski Partizana* (Moscow-Leningrad, 1925), p. 104.
[10] Zobachev, in *Za Vlast Sovietov*, p. 21.
[11] Matsakov and Turunov, *Khronika Grazhdanskoi Voiny* (Moscow-Leningrad, 1926), p. 80. Zobachev, in *Z.V.S.*, p. 25.
[12] Dimitriev, in *Z.V.S.*, p. 45.

breakdown of communications between Party centres within Siberia.[13] Similarly, the Ural-Siberian Buro drew up and issued organizational directives: e.g. a Supreme Staff to take charge of all military activities was to be set up within the Siberian Regional Committee of the Party. Provincial staffs were to be set up within Provincial Committees, each containing seven departments with specialized functions.[14] There were detailed instructions regarding Partisan detachments.[15] But whether these or other Party directives ever reached, or influenced, those who were actually conducting Partisan operations is open to considerable doubt. On February 1 the Party launched a second rising in Omsk, resulting like the first in a costly defeat.

In late March, the Third All-Siberian Underground Bolshevik Congress was held in Omsk and attended by delegates not only from Siberia proper but from Trans-Baikalia and the Far East as well. Obviously some of those present had received the directives of the Ural-Siberian Buro, which are reflected in the elaborate and ambitious resolutions which the Congress passed—covering every possible aspect of organization, mobilization, armament, communications and tactics, and calling for contact to be established with 'the Communists of America, Japan and China'. In sharp contrast to these resolutions are the reports from the visiting delegates, which make it clear that nowhere throughout the vast area was there effective Party activity, or, indeed, appreciable Party membership. A similar impression is made by the report of a Partisan representatives' congress, held shortly afterwards in Tomsk.[16] But these were the last underground congresses to be held for some time. Within a month the whole of the Omsk Committee had been arrested and shot. Apart from Omsk there had been Bolshevik sponsored revolts in Kansk, Krasnoiarsk, Tomsk, Tiumen and other centres. All had ended in defeat, heavy casualties, arrests and the disruption of the local Party organization. The brave but ill-judged decision in favour of local risings had resulted, by May 1919, in the virtual extinction of the Bolshevik underground. In the words of a Soviet writer, 'the convulsive movements of the town proletariat were liquidated to the root and left no noticeable mark behind them on the social struggle of the epoch.'[17] It is true that individual Bolsheviks played an

[13] Matsakov and Turunov, *Khronika*, p. 276.
[14] Document in *Z.V.S.*, p. 314.   [15] Document in *Z.V.S.*, pp. 314-15.
[16] Bykov and Raivid, *Kolchakovshchina* (Ekaterinburg, 1924), pp. 164-86. Zobachev, in *Z.V.S.*, p. 31. Dimitriev, in *Z.V.S.*, pp. 47, 48. Rabochaia, *Revoliutsia na Urale* (Ekaterinburg, 1921), pp. 177-80.
[17] V. Eltsin, in *Proletarskaia Revoliutsia*, No. 50 (1926), p. 79.

important part in many of the Partisan movements. But they did so as individuals. Subsequent claims that the movements were launched and led by the Party as such are untenable. 'Peasants neither asked for nor expected help from the towns. They were suspicious of anything that came from the towns, including the proletariat. This cut away the ground from under the feet of the Communist Party in attempts to organize and control the movement.'[18]

(v)

Ever since the revolution of February 1917 the Siberian peasant had been almost completely exempt from town-based administrative interference or control. He had come to acquire a vested interest in this freedom, to feel he had a moral right to it. Furthermore, the reported frequent changes of government gave the impression that government stability and effectiveness were things of the past. We hear of peasants in the Barnaul area refusing, in July 1918, to pay taxes because 'the new government has only been for a short time in existence.'[19] The demand for taxes, the call-up to the Siberian and later to the Kolchak armies, the requisitioning of horses and farm property, were all things to be automatically resisted. The arrival of enforcement squads and punitive expeditions and the haphazard brutality of their methods created a profound shock. There were of course other factors. Parts of the Altai and Yenisei provinces suffered severely from the loss of their export markets.[20] There was a widespread jealousy and hatred of the privileged and pro-Kolchak Cossack settlements. There was, here and there, the element of banditry and 'hooliganism'. There was the resentment (later a problem for Partisan administrations) at endeavours to suppress private distillation of vodka.[21] All over the Siberian countryside the stage was set for incidents, and hundreds of incidents did occur. Most of them petered out. But where the peasants found a leader—a fugitive Bolshevik with his sense of devotion and discipline or an ex-non-commissioned officer who knew how to fight—there was the beginning of a Partisan band. And where there was some initial victory over the local police or garrison, enough to give rise to the hope that the area could be freed and could be held, there came a rush of recruits alike from Starozhili with something to

[18] V. Eltsin, in *Proletarskaia Revoliutsia*, No. 50 (1926), p. 80.
[19] *Id.*, p. 56.   [20] *Id.*, No. 49 (1926), p. 10.
[21] It was estimated that in the Yenisei Province 2½ poods of grain per year per head of population went into illegal stills—Kolosov, *Sibir pri Kolchake* (Petrograd, 1923), p. 29.

defend and from Novoseli with nothing to lose; and the movement was launched. But its inception, in every case, arose from local, fortuitous circumstances. Mamontov, an ex-N.C.O. and well-to-do farmer in the Altai Province, received what he considered an unjustified tax demand. In the course of the quarrel he killed the tax collector and escaped to the taiga—thus starting the career which led to his becoming Commander-in-Chief of the Peasant Armies of the Altai.[22]

(vi)

Yakovenko was a native of Taseevo.[23] His parents died when he was a child and he was brought up by relatives. He had no schooling, but taught himself to read and write. He became a skilled carpenter and also owned a farm of his own with four horses. He was thus a middle peasant. He was called up for military service in 1914. He won three George Crosses and was made an N.C.O. In July 1917 he came home on leave. Taseevo was a big village and there was some political activity, with keen rivalry between the 150 Socialist Revolutionaries and the 135 Bolsheviks. Yakovenko took some time to make his mind up, but finally joined the Bolsheviks. In October his army leave expired and he was posted to a unit in Kansk, where he became a member of the local Soviet of Workers and Soldiers. The next six weeks were occupied in work against the Socialist Revolutionaries, who were manoeuvring to win over the local garrison. However, in November the Bolshevik Military Revolutionary Committee succeeded in disbanding the garrison. Yakovenko was demobilized in December and became a full-time Party worker. He spent the winter and spring in and around his native Taseevo—his tasks being to form a Red Militia, to substitute Soviets for the local government organs set up under the Provisional Government and to wage an all-out war against speculation and private stills. All this turned out to be difficult, but he eventually got together a force of some sixty men—mostly unarmed. His first reaction to the Czech occupation of Kansk was to march on the town and join up with other Red detachments in driving the Czechs out. By the time he had collected arms for his force he heard of the Bolshevik collapse at Krasnoiarsk. He decided to go north-west to the Red garrison at Yeniseisk. News came that Yeniseisk had also fallen. Organized resistance now seemed hopeless so he disbanded his force and went back to Taseevo. In July a White security squad

[22] V. Eltsin, in *Borba za Ural i Sibir* (Moscow-Leningrad, 1926), p. 273.
[23] For following pages, Yakovenko, *op. cit.*, pp. 9-20.

arrived in the village to arrest him, but he escaped to the taiga. It was here, in November, that he received an order from the Party Committee at Kansk to start a revolt. The order seemed to him nonsense and he took no action. By December it was too cold to stay in the open and he hid in cottages of friends, first in a village near Fanachet and later in Taseevo. Here he conceived the idea of capturing the village. He assembled, conspiratorially, some twenty helpers and the coup was successfully carried out at the turn of the year. The Taseevo revolt had started. By the end of January the Taseevo insurgent army numbered 218 men. Between twenty and thirty had rifles, the others shot-guns. A staff of six was elected to take charge of all civil and military affairs. They were Yakovenko himself, three rich peasants, a political exile and the son of the manager of the local salt works. Three of the five were Party members or sympathizers. Two had served at the front and been made N.C.O.s. One held the George Cross.

Up to the end of February the Taseevtsi defeated four successive White expeditions despatched against them. During the comparative lull of the next three months they absorbed five smaller Partisan 'fronts', and their operations extended from near the Trans-Siberian railway in the south to the river Angara in the north, and from the Yenisei river in the east to the neighbourhood of Taishet. But they were unable to withstand the big White offensive of June. Taseevo was abandoned, and the Partisans with their wives and dependants, the sick and the aged and a hundred stretcher cases from the hospital retreated for some 150 miles into the taiga. By mid-July a new front was more or less stabilized, the Whites on the west bank of the river Usolka and the Partisans on the east bank. In September they reoccupied Taseevo. Thereafter their pressure grew progressively stronger, until in December the collapse of the Kolchak regime opened the way to Kansk.

(vii)

Shchetinkin was born in 1885, the son of a poor peasant near Riazan. As a boy he went to Moscow and worked for a carpenter. He was called up for military service in 1906 and posted to a unit near Achinsk. When passed to the reserve in 1909 he decided to settle in Siberia, married a local girl and set up as a carpenter in her native village of Krasnovka. He did not prosper, so went back to the army and was admitted to a training school for N.C.O.s. On the outbreak of war he was a sergeant-major. He showed exceptional gallantry on the German front, was awarded four George Crosses and successively promoted up to the rank of captain. In late 1916 he was made instructor at a military training establishment in Siberia. In his own words he 'took no active part in the February and October revolutions.' He was, however, prepared to serve the new government of Russia. In March 1918 he became head of the criminal investigation department of the Achinsk police under the Bolsheviks; and at the same time he was enrolled as a Party member. On the Czech overturn he was ordered by the Party to take command of a scratch force of foreign P.O.W.s and drive out the Czechs. The force was weak in numbers and ill-armed; and the venture appeared both to Shchetinkin and his rank and file to be too hopeless to be attempted.[24] The P.O.W.s dispersed and Shchetinkin himself hid in the taiga to escape arrest by the Whites. His family brought him food. As winter came on he was forced to leave his hiding place by wolves. (His family could have found him a gun, but shots would have alerted the Security Police.)

He came back to Krasnovka, and hid in a garret in his own house. When he smoked the smell of tobacco came through the chinks and made the children inquisitive. Once his little daughter saw him, but though questioned by the police she denied any knowledge of her father.[25]

One market day in Achinsk in December 1918 a Kolchak militia man told a peasant that the security force was planning to arrest some sixty peasants in neighbouring villages, eighteen of them—including Shchetinkin's brother-in-law—in Krasnovka. News came back to the men concerned, and Shchetinkin held a secret meeting. It was agreed to go into the taiga and become 'self-defenders'. Touch was established with neighbouring villages and ninety men assembled at the rendezvous. Shchetinkin was elected military commander. Within a few days the numbers had grown to 200, of whom some 30% had rifles. A White force came out from Achinsk and was defeated —partly by the skilful use of the Partisan ski detachment.[26] Among the spoils of victory were 20,000 rounds of small arms ammunition. A congress was then called, attended by peasant delegates from nine volosts, which elected an Executive Committee consisting of Shchetinkin and two of his fighting men, and village representatives.[27] Resolutions were passed calling

[24] P. E. Shchetinkin, *Borba s Kolchakovshchinoi* (Novosibirsk, 1919)—Foreword by Vegman, pp. 8-9.
[25] Vassa Shchetinkin (Shchetinkin's widow), in *Z.V.S.*, pp. 191-4.
[26] P. Shchetinkin, *Borba s Kolchakovshchinoi* (Novosibirsk, 1929), pp. 15-23.
[27] *Id.*, pp. 26-8.

for more volunteers, for the call-up of local 'frontovniks', and for 'self-taxation' in order to provide supplies and uniforms. It was also decided to stop the sending of produce to Achinsk or other towns, and to fix prices in the villages. Further resolutions called for the raising of the cultural level of the district and for the maintenance of roads and bridges.

It was a spirited beginning. But the movement was operating far too close to the vital main railway line to be accorded any respite by the Kolchak government. In mid-March four White columns converged upon the area. After a week of skirmishing and fighting Partisan ammunition ran short (as so often happened) and the position was hopeless. A council of war at Krasnovka rejected a proposal to disperse into the taiga and adopted Shchetinkin's project to break through the ring. The Partisans with their trains of carts and their families set out westwards, overran a small White contingent and captured 30,000 rounds of ammunition. They turned south, crossed the railway, dispersing two armoured trains by means of a ruse, and then made west-south-west as far as Tisul, beating off a White attack at Berezovskoe. At Tisul they turned south-east, crossed the Yenisei after more fighting near Novoselovo, and made east towards Stepnoi-Badzhei. There was some alarm at Kravchenko's headquarters at the reported approach of this unknown armed force,[28] but an advance party on skis were able to explain matters. On April 17 the main body (or what was left of it after their four hundred mile trek) arrived at Kravchenko's outposts and were received with gifts of bread. Agreement was soon reached between the two commanders. The newcomers were incorporated into the Stepnoi-Badzhei army as the North Achinsk Partisan Regiment. Shchetinkin was elected regimental commander. Sick and wounded were admitted to the Stepnoi-Badzhei hospital. Non-combatants were allotted jobs according to their qualifications, and all money and stores handed over to the United Soviet.[29]

(viii)

Kravchenko came of a family of prosperous peasants. He served in the Imperial Army and was promoted to lieutenant. He seems to have returned to Siberia in 1917, and, under the first Bolshevik period, to have had some connection with the Red Militia. But, in spite of what is claimed in later Soviet build-ups, the Whites apparently did not consider him suffi-

[28] Kravchenko, in *Z.V.S.*, p. 220.
[29] Shchetinkin, *op. cit.*, pp. 31, 32; see also Shchetinkin, in *Z.V.S.*, pp. 177-9.

ciently tainted to warrant arrest, and throughout the summer of 1918 he was working his own farm in the Zamanie area (south-east of Krasnoiarsk and south-west of Kansk). The Zamanie peasants had a tradition of resistance to authority. Mobilization and requisition orders from Omsk only tended to make the peasants bellicose. Kravchenko records: 'At the end of October representatives of local peasants came to my farm and suggested starting an armed insurrection. I came to Stepnoi-Badzhei where we had a meeting with delegates from other villages. It was decided that when Stepnoi-Badzhei gave the word all should assemble with arms at a given point. It was also decided to establish contact with Krasnoiarsk.'[30]

In late November came news that a punitive detachment of White militia were on their way to occupy the area: whereupon a group of eighteen peasants seized Stepnoi-Badzhei and sent a message to Kravchenko to come and assume command. In mid-December the Partisan force numbered fifty-three men. The first brush with the Whites took place on December 20-21: the Partisans captured two machine guns, a number of rifles and much ammunition. Victory brought a boom in recruiting. On January 1-3 the Whites were again defeated (their Colonel was subsequently relieved of his command for incompetence) and a week later Partisan fighting strength had risen to 536. In mid-January they scored their third victory. The Stepnoi-Badzhei movement was now a force to be reckoned with.[31]

Kravchenko writes: 'When our rising started we sent comrades to Krasnoiarsk to contact the Bolshevik Party Committee there. We hoped that the Krasnoiarsk railway workers would support us. But Kolchak concentrated big forces in the towns and his Security Service shot or imprisoned the best Party workers. In view of this we had to rely solely on our own strength.'[32] And so in March the Partisan Army Congress proclaimed the establishment of the 'Soviet Republic of Stepnoi-Badzhei', with Kravchenko as Commander-in-Chief, and arranged for the election of a United Soviet, including representatives of fourteen volosts, as supreme civil authority.[33] By the time of Shchetinkin's arrival in late April the young republic had a working administration. The fighting strength amounted to 2,700 infantry and 350 cavalry with a special machine gun section. In addition there was a labour force of prisoners-of-war amounting to 1,500 men.[34]

[30] Kravchenko, in *Z.V.S.*, p. 214 (from a shortened version of an unfinished manuscript memoir by Kravchenko in the Party archives at Novosibirsk).
[31] Kravchenko, in *Z.V.S.*, pp. 215-17. [32] *Id.*, p. 217. [33] *Id.*, p. 218 n. [34] *Id.*, p. 219.

As elsewhere the spring marked a comparative lull in active operations. There were sporadic sabotage forays against the main railway line. Touch was established by courier with the Taseevo Partisans; and a scheme was mooted (but did not materialize) for a joint attack on Kansk. On the White side the Czechs and other Allied contingents were taking over guard duties along the railway, and General Rozanov was preparing for the major offensive. Kravchenko sent delegates to Czech units in the hope of securing Czech neutrality. But they had no success.[35]

In late May the White forces (estimated by the Partisans to number 12,000 men) began their advance. The Partisans ran short of ammunition. An order was issued: 'on June 14 the hospitals and all offices and installations will evacuate Stepnoi-Badzhei and move into the depths of the taiga . . . a retreat in the same direction will take place along the whole front.'[36] Shchetinkin gives the ultimate destination as Vernyi[37]; but a more immediate attraction was the hope that once in the frontier area it would be possible to buy arms and ammunition from the Mongols or else, through Mongol intermediaries, from China.[38]

The long trek southwards was hard and arduous. Just as Partisan armies swell with victory they fritter away in defeat. Many men lose heart; others are unwilling to move any distance from their homes and farms. In course of the first forty miles of retreat the Stepnoi-Badzhei Army lost 60% of its effectives. Staff and command were drastically reorganized and a 'military dictatorship' instituted to enforce discipline. The retreat continued through the taiga and along mountain tracks. With the army, now numbering little over a thousand (and according to some accounts far less) were 250 sick and wounded from the hospital and some three thousand dependants, refugees and prisoners.[39] There were occasional brushes with small White detachments and one or two lucky windfalls of arms and supplies. At the end of July Belotsarsk (Kyzyl) the capital of Uriankhai (Tanu-Tuva) was occupied without fighting. Here the Partisans set up their hospital and cartridge factory and paused to rest and refit.[40]

[35] Kravchenko, in Z.V.S., p. 221.
[36] Id., p. 223.
[37] Shchetinkin, op. cit., pp. 38, 39. (Vernyi is now Alma Ata.)
[38] Kravchenko, in Z.V.S., p. 224.
[39] Id., p. 224. (See also Eltsin, in Prol. Rev., No. 49 (1926), p. 30.)
[40] Much of the factory and the chief mechanic were unfortunately lost when two poods of gunpowder were accidentally exploded—Karasev, in Z.V.S., p. 237.

Uriankhai was in a state of anarchy with the native Tanu-Tuvans in revolt and with various Mongol princes trying to exploit the collapse of Russian power to enlarge their territories. With one such prince Kravchenko and Shchetinkin started to negotiate: their request for permission to pass through Mongolia to Turkestan was referred back to Urga.[41] In late August a White Cossack force arrived from the north to retake the area. There was a sharp engagement in which the Partisans lost 37 killed and 44 wounded; but the Whites were decisively defeated and withdrew in confusion. The Mongols, who had been sitting on the fence, presented gifts to the victorious leaders and gave permission to pass through Mongol territory.[42] However, Partisan morale was now restored, and there were more attractive objectives nearer home. On September 3 they started North again. Ten days later they captured Minusinsk with trifling loss. Thereafter, as the White administration crumbled, their progress was a triumphal march. By the end of November their force numbered 18,000 men with five field guns and 153 machine guns. On December 22 they contacted reconnaissance units of the Red Army. On the 24th they captured Achinsk. And on January 7 and 8 a formal session with Red Army representatives at Krasnoiarsk decided that the Partisan Peasant Army should be formed into the 1st Yenisei Rifle Division of the regular Red forces.[43]

(ix)

Partisan problems of supply and the methods devised to solve them are well illustrated in Yakovenko's memoirs. At first there was no difficulty over village produce. There were large stocks of grain and leather in Taseevo when it was taken. And peasant enthusiasm for the cause of freedom, stimulated by agitators from Yakovenko's staff, brought a stream of cartloads of free-will offerings.[44] Once the movement was established a system of 'self-taxation' was introduced in all areas. The big White offensive of the summer of 1919 of course made things far more difficult. When the Partisans came back to Taseevo in September the village was a burnt out shell. Requisitioning committees had to be set up in order to keep the forces fed. And the interruption of land work and the removal or death of so many of the villagers raised anxiety for food supply in the future. Partisans were seconded from combatant service and set to work in squads on the harvest and on autumn sowing. Shortage of

[41] Kravchenko, in *Z.V.S.*, p. 227. [42] *Id.*, pp. 231, 232.
[43] Shchetinkin, *op. cit.*, p. 62. [44] Yakovenko, *op. cit.*, p. 56.

cattle was met as far as possible by organizing raids on White-held territory.[45]

Winter clothing was of course a first essential for campaigning in a Siberian winter. Partisan records contain frequent and urgent references to the making up of boots and clothing. At the threat of a shortage of material in the Taseevo area Yakovenko's staff ordered a census of dogs. One dog might be retained by each household. The others were slaughtered and their skins made into coats and caps. The appearance, Yakovenko tells us, was curious. But they kept the wearers warm.[46]

The most urgent military necessity was small arms ammunition of which there was never sufficient. A certain amount was obtained by capture. Quite early on an order was issued by the Stepnoi-Badzhei command that all ammunition captured was not to be retained by the captors but must be handed over to the regimental Soviet, who would arrange for its distribution—priority going to machine gun detachments.[47] There were occasional opportunities of obtaining small supplies by purchase. But right from the beginning all the more important movements started their own factories or workshops for the manufacture of cartridges.[48] That at Stepnoi-Badzhei was run by a technician, referred to by Kravchenko as 'our saviour' who was sent out by the Krasnoiarsk Bolsheviks[49] and who seems to have been their only tangible contribution to the Partisan cause. He took part in the retreat and was subsequently killed in an explosion at Belotsarsk. Taseevo had a technician from Western Russia. This primitive manufacture was very much a matter of trial and error. There were frequent accidents and casualties both in the workshops and in the field. But improvement came with experience, and by the end it was claimed that most Partisans had some confidence in the home made product.[50] These workshops also repaired rifles, and we even hear of attempts at the manufacture of home made artillery. There was one Konkorin, a Petrograd metal worker, who produced nine muzzle loading cannons for the Zimino Partisans in the Altai. It was claimed (twenty-five years after the event) that they functioned satisfactorily.[51] A report dated nearer to the time of fighting comes from a participant in the campaign along the river Angara in the far north. 'At the taking of Ust-Kut we had on our side a battery consisting of one home made

[45] *Id.*, pp. 65, 66.   [46] *Id.*, p. 42.
[47] Karasev, in *Z.V.S.*, p. 237.
[48] Kantyshev, in *Prol. Rev.*, No. 22 (1923), p. 175.
[49] Karasev, in *Z.V.S.*, p. 237.   [50] Yakovenko, *op. cit.*, pp. 58-61.
[51] Arkhipov, in *Z.V.S.*, p. 81.

cannon. It did not work, but the noise and rumble, when stuffed with a great deal of powder, served to frighten the enemy.'[52]

(x)

Throughout the Civil War in the east medical and hospital conditions were appalling; and in the Partisan areas they were inevitably more primitive than elsewhere. It is an illustration of the exclusively peasant nature of the insurrections and of the gap between the villages and the towns that although anti-Kolchak feeling was fairly widespread among the professional classes there seems to be no recorded instance of a doctor coming out, of his own free will, to help the Partisans. Then there was peasant ignorance and peasant prejudice in matters medical. There has been preserved an appeal from a group near Shitkino (east of Taseevo) for supplies of vodka as a preventive against small pox.[53] The *bona fides* of this appeal is open to doubt and it was almost certainly refused. But the importance attached by the Partisan leaders to their medical services comes out clearly.

One of the first acts of the Stepnoi-Badzhei command under Kravchenko was to set up a hospital which, it was claimed, could look after 300 patients.[54] We are told nothing about the staffing of it. Yakovenko at Taseevo had a hospital of thirty beds with a couple of feldshers (medical assistants) to carry out major operations. In one of his raids to the north he captured a 'real doctor', and made full use of him for the next few weeks. But then the doctor bolted back to the Whites. It is certain that something of what was lacking in skill and equipment was made up by devotion. No pains were spared to save the wounded from their probable fate if captured by the Kolchak forces. As we have seen, all stretcher cases were successfully evacuated from both Stepnoi-Badzhei and Taseevo at the time of the White offensives, in spite of the enormous physical difficulties. Yakovenko was obviously proud of his hospital and claims that the death rate was only 2% of surgical cases and 5% of typhus cases. The rate was probably higher than that, and it is fairly certain that numbers must have died before they ever got to hospital. But even so there remains a considerable achievement. Yakovenko ascribes it partly to the healthy pinewood air.[55] But much was doubtless due to the inherent toughness of the patients.

---

[52] Brun, in *Prol. Rev.*, No. 38 (1925), p. 234.
[53] Maksakov and Turunov, *Partizanskoe Dvizhenie*, p. 275.
[54] Kravchenko, in *Z.V.S.*, p. 218.   [55] Yakovenko, *op. cit.*, p. 62.

(xi)

It was obviously important to be kept informed of White military dispositions and intentions. There were of course sufficient Partisan sympathizers in White-held villages to ensure a flow of intelligence, albeit often garbled and inaccurate, by peasant bush telegraph. Taseevo established and maintained a secret underground network in Kansk.[56] Stepnoi-Badzhei seems to have had some intermittent contacts with Krasnoiarsk. A more important source of information was unwittingly provided by the Kolchak military. It was unsafe to send single despatch riders through disaffected country areas, and to provide an adequate body-guard would involve too much manpower Communications from White headquarters to outlying posts were accordingly encyphered, sealed in bags, and handed to a peasant who was promised a reward of, say, 200 roubles on safe delivery to the addressee. The peasant would hand the bag to the Partisans who would open, copy the contents, re-seal, and hand back to the peasant for delivery to the Kolchak outpost. At Yakovenko's staff was one Treumann, an old Party member from Latvia, who knew something of cryptography and had no difficulty in breaking the White codes.[57] Later on, when the Kolchak regime was disintegrating, intelligence problems, like so many others, became easy to solve. It frequently happened that a White village or outpost would be overrun without the knowledge of higher White formations further back. The telegraph staff were naturally anxious to ingratiate themselves with their new masters; and the Partisans were therefore able to tap out conversations on the direct line with the unsuspecting White command.[58]

(xii)

All Partisan movements, at a comparatively early stage, were faced with the problem of finance. There is no record of any cash contribution from Russia having reached any of the main forces in the field; and a striking illustration of the inability of the Party to help the Partisans is that the Taseevo movement had to maintain, at their own expense, the underground espionage and purchasing organization in Kansk. There were a number of necessities which it was impossible to produce in the villages; and throughout the Kolchak epoch there was an extensive black market in most of the main centres. In the spring of 1919 a rifle could be had in Kansk for 100 roubles, a

[56] *Id.*, p. 56.   [57] *Id.*, pp. 39, 40.
[58] Brun, in *Proletarska Revoliutsia*, No. 30 (1925), p. 234.

revolver for 80, and ammunition, of which the supply was limited, at ten rounds for a rouble. It was in Kansk that the Taseevo group bought caps for their home-made cartridges, medical supplies, and any complicated pieces of equipment required.[59]

The outlay on such imports, however, was small in comparison with the internal expenditure involved as each movement developed into a government in miniature with military and civilian establishments. In the first flush of enthusiasm there were voluntary contributions in cash as well as in kind. Then there was the confiscation of the property of White adherents. In the untidy beginnings of some of the Altai bands this was apt to lead to friction. We hear of Gromov being faced with a mutiny because of his refusal to share out funds, confiscated to finance his campaign, among the members of his troop.[60] At one stage, when civilian courts got going, some revenue accrued from fines imposed for various offences. A far more important source was, of course, the 'self taxation', to be described in a later section. Towards the end of the period, in the autumn and winter of 1919, the bulk of the funds were obtained from areas held by the Whites. Yakovenko's group brought the seizure of Kolchak taxes to a fine art. Watch would be kept, by sympathizers among the minor White officials, on outlying tax offices, and as soon as their balances warranted they were raided. A certificate of confiscation, giving details of the sums concerned, was always forwarded afterwards to the local Director of Taxes.

Even larger sums were collected by the raising of Partisan loans in White-occupied territory. There were dangers involved, as subscribers no less than collectors were given, if caught, short shrift by the Kolchak Security Service. But, especially towards the end, there were compensating inducements for the subscriber. It seemed a means of re-insuring with the Reds. And as the Omsk rouble progressively and rapidly depreciated it might well be the only way of keeping any money at all. The total obtained by the Taseevo group by means of Partisan loans amounted to more than two million roubles.[61]

(xiii)

Partisan organization was simple, spontaneous and generally democratic. The original little group would elect a leader. As recruits came in, a mass meeting would elect a Supreme Staff and a Supreme Commander—this last being usually the ori-

[59] Yakovenko, *op. cit.*, p. 56.   [60] Eltsin, in *Prol. Rev.*, No. 50 (1926), p. 57.
[61] Yakovenko, *op. cit.*, pp. 57-8.

ginal founder of the movement. In due course the fighting men were split up into units. Thus the Taseevo Army eventually consisted of three infantry regiments each of three battalions, each battalion consisting of three companies of 70 to 100 men. Attached to each regimental headquarters was a reconnaissance group, numbering about sixty, of whom some were mounted. There were four cavalry regiments, each of four squadrons of 70 to 100 men. There was also a machine gun detachment and a special operations detachment directly subordinated to the Supreme Staff. In all battalions and companies there were elected committees or soviets who looked after such matters as the distribution of rations and clothing. They had also the power to try minor breaches of discipline and award punishments up to eight additional fatigues. All such decisions required confirmation by the battalion commander.[62]

In the Taseevo movement the Supreme Staff exercised civilian as well as military powers until after the big White offensive of the summer. In July, when the front had been stabilized, an Army Congress was called which elected an Army Soviet of six to act as supreme executive.[63] In Stepnoi-Badzhei an Army Congress had elected an Army Soviet as early as January 1919. Purely military affairs were left to the Supreme Staff. There were regimental soviets and regimental courts, with a supreme Military Court on the level of the Supreme Staff.[64] In March, as we have seen, a republic was proclaimed and a United Soviet was set up as supreme executive. The Army Soviet remained in being, at any rate for a time; and in April a Peasant Congress was held, as civilian counterpart to the Army Congress.

In the Altai various groups operated independently throughout the summer, their respective staffs controlling both civil and military affairs. In early September the three most important groups, commanded respectively by Mamontov, Gromov and Arkhipov, united to form the 'Peasant Red Army'. Two days later 400 delegates representing the Novonikolaevsk, Barnaul, Kamen and Slavgorod departments, set up a Regional Executive Committee as the paramount civil authority.[65] Both the Supreme Staff of the new united Red Peasant Army and the Regional Executive Committee had subordinate bodies— Military Revolutionary Staffs and Executive Committees at district (raion) and subdistrict (volost) levels.[66]

[62] *Id.*, pp. 54, 55.   [63] *Id.*, pp. 38-9.
[64] Kravchenko, in *Z.V.S.*, pp. 217, 218.
[65] Gromov, in *Z.V.S.*, pp. 59-60. Arkhipov, in *Z.V.S.*, pp. 91-2.
[66] Kantyshev, in *Prol. Rev.*, No. 22 (1923), p. 173.

(xiv)

An interesting illustration of the way in which Partisan government worked is in the fairly full account which has survived of the First Peasant Congress of the Kansk, Krasnoiarsk and Achinsk departments, held in the Stepnoi-Badzhei area from April 25 to April 30, 1919.[67] It was opened by speeches from the two military commanders, Kravchenko and the newly arrived Shchetinkin, who reported on recent military operations, described the position on the Partisan front, and called for full support from villages in the rear. The civilian chairman of the Congress made a suitable reply, but there was little further rhetoric, and the Congress proceeded to get through an impressive volume of business.

The first item was finance and supply. It was first suggested that each peasant be left enough grain for his subsistence and his sowing, and that all over and above this amount be registered and held at the disposition of the United Soviet. There was strong opposition to this, and the matter was referred to a commission of twelve peasants (representing twelve volosts), two front-line Partisans, and one member of the general public (of whom unfortunately no details are recorded). In due course the commission recommended a 'self tax' of 5% of all grain and 3% of all horned cattle. If these rates were found insufficient they were to be increased by $2\frac{1}{2}$% and 1% respectively. A small tax should also be levied on property other than horned cattle and grain. Provision was made for a special form of tax on the earnings of artisans and craftsmen, and for concessions to the sick, the aged and the front-line fighters. Tax collection was to be supervised by local committees. These proposals were debated and finally carried by 54 votes to 49.

Other items to be dealt with included the medical service, the treatment to be accorded to refugees, migration and land allocations. An important task, again entrusted to a special commission, was the fixing of prices for essential goods and foodstuffs and for essential services. Thus rye was fixed at 7 to 8 roubles per pood, wheat 10 to 12, beef 35 to 40; and butter at 3 roubles a pound. The charge for milling grain was fixed at one pound of grain per pood milled; for making a pair of boots (sapogi) at 20 roubles. Where no specific figure was laid down for the job the charge for skilled labour was 2 to $2\frac{1}{2}$ roubles per hour. A man's basic monthly ration was established as one pood of flour and 15 pounds of meat.

[67] Maksakov and Turunov, *Partizanskoe Dvizhenie*, pp. 129-43.

Much time was devoted to the matter of Partisan courts. In particular there was the question of capital punishment and there was strong pressure for its total abolition. But in the end the argument of military necessity prevailed, and the final decision was that the Army Soviet and that body only might pronounce a death sentence.

Meanwhile another commission worked out a scale of appropriate punishments for crimes likely to come before the civilian Partisan courts. There were, of course, no facilities for imprisonment, and the normal alternative to a fine was a spell of unpaid labour on behalf of the community. Thus it was laid down that a conviction for being drunk and disorderly entailed a fine of 25 to 100 roubles, or ten to thirty days' labour. Habitual drunks who wasted their subsistence and failed to support their families were liable to labour for an indefinite period. Gaming and card playing entailed two weeks' to one year's labour and confiscation of the cards and stakes. Murder when drunk, rape or theft (other than theft of horses)—from three years' labour upwards. Speculation in foodstuffs—one to five years' labour plus a fine of 300 to 10,000 roubles. Really serious crimes, such as deliberate murder, murder with robbery, arson or horse stealing were to be passed to the Military Courts. An 'improper attitude' (nedobrosovestnoe otnoshenie) to elected officials in the course of their duties called for one month to three years' labour; slandering any authority set up by the revolutionary movement—from one to five years. But, 'if any one noticed malpractices on the part of elected officials, the matter should be brought to the attention of the appropriate authority.'

The Congress closed with the election of delegates to serve on the United Soviet. One of the successful candidates complained he was the victim of malicious rumours (their nature is not recorded) and asked for an enquiry. The enquiry was held, and he was completely exonerated. Another of those elected, Comrade Nizotsev, asked to be excused from serving on the Soviet as he was too busy at home. This plea was not accepted and Comrade Nizotsev was informed that he should serve; but he was allotted one prisoner-of-war to help him on his farm.

(xv)

Partisan news sheets and pamphlets began to appear very soon. The first Stepnoi-Badzhei 'newspaper', *Krestianskaia Pravda*, started very early in 1919.[68] Already in January Kravchenko's agents were trying to distribute multigraphed copies

---

[68] Kravchenko, in *Z.V.S.*, p. 220.

of the following appeal to young recruits of the Kolchak forces in the Krasnoiarsk area: 'Go home. Endeavour to take your rifles with you. By joining up with us you will be freed from all military obligations. We look after our young brothers. They and the children must be preserved for building up the future. The only ones among us who fight the enemy with arms on our front are our brothers and fathers who fought against the Germans.'[69] Proclamations to the civilian inhabitants of newly invaded districts emphasized the friendliness of Partisan intentions and the good behaviour of the Partisan rank and file.[70] Almost every Partisan group of any size had one or more newspapers. One or two had printing presses; the other productions were simple affairs, typewritten or multigraphed, on one or two sheets and appearing at irregular intervals. They were important as providers of news at a time when Siberian villages had never heard of such a thing as W/T reception. The news was not always accurate: the Taseevo *Izvestia* announced the capture of Chelyabinsk by the Red Army in February 1919, over six months before the event.[71] But no doubt the item served to maintain morale, as did the more circumstantial and accurate account in the same issue of the local Partisan victory over the Whites at Khristo-Rozhdestvensko. This maintenance of morale and with it the maintenance of discipline were two of the major problems of the conduct of a campaign on the democratic Partisan lines. 'Panic-mongering' and 'non-fulfilment of duties' are featured among surviving records of the proceedings of Partisan courts.[72] But sanctions, in the loose and democratic Partisan armies, could only be applied when they had the approval of the great majority of the rank and file. Otherwise the army would dissolve. It is reasonably safe to assume that the only groups that managed to survive and to develop into appreciable movements were those with leaders whose personalities were such as to ensure some level of morale and discipline. A striking example of the very many incipient movements that came to nothing, for lack of such qualities, is the fiasco at Yeniseisk. The garrison of 250 defected, the governor and his officers were removed, the town occupied. The new Partisan/ Mutineer masters of Yeniseisk issued a few proclamations and dug a few trenches round the outskirts. But they then proceeded to get drunk and stayed drunk; so that a small White detach-

---

[69] Maksakov and Turunov, *Partizanskoe Dvizhenie*, p. 62.

[70] E.g. proclamation issued by Kravchenko and Shchetinkin in the Minusinsk area, reproduced in *Z.V.S.*, p. 184. See also proclamation in *Z.V.S.*, p. 326.

[71] Maksakov and Turunov, *Partizanskoe Dvizhenie*, pp. 54-5.

[72] *Id.*, pp. 252-4.

ment that came up from Krasnoiarsk a fortnight later was able to crush the revolt in a matter of hours with no casualty beyond one soldier wounded.[73]

(xvi)

It has always been an axiom of the Bolshevik Party that Party work and ideological instruction are the best safeguards for morale and discipline. And it is significant that even where Party members were in positions of command Party work in the various movements was almost completely neglected till the autumn of 1919. The autumn of course was a difficult time for discipline: Partisan defeats in the big White offensives of the summer had placed a severe strain on the original armies, and the turn of the tide in September had occasioned a flood of very miscellaneous and often almost unmanageable recruits. It was in September that the Supreme Staff at Taseevo compiled a list of old Party workers in the villages in their area and started a campaign of ideological education.[74] Care was taken to avoid offending peasant susceptibilities, for instance anti-religious agitation was soft pedalled.[75] A little later Taseevo started military schools, one for Partisan officers and one for N.C.O.s, and Marxist instruction formed part of the curriculum.[76] In the Altai little or nothing was done until the unification of the three main groups in September. Then an Agitation Section was set up, originally subordinated to the Supreme Staff and later to the Regional Executive Committee. Its head was one Koltsov, a labourer from Petrograd. Under him were 'twenty fighting agitators. Most of them were simple people. They had no political education and knew little about socialism, but they believed in socialism and were whole-heartedly devoted to it.'[77] A month later, largely at the instance of Arkhipov, a regional Party headquarters was set up in the Regional Executive Committee, and efforts were made to organize Party cells in the villages. At the same time Political Commissars were appointed to the various Partisan regiments. It is claimed that they did good service. But after the final defeat of Kolchak, one of them, Plotnikov, Commissar of the 1st Altai regiment, formed a band of his own and fought against the Bolsheviks.[78]

(xvii)

In any consideration of Partisan aims it is necessary once again to remember the isolation of the various movements from

---

[73] Maksakov and Turunov, *Partizanskoe Dvizhenie*, pp. 83-5. Yakovenko, *op. cit.*, p. 29.   [74] Yakovenko, *op. cit.*, pp. 71, 72.   [75] *Id.*, p. 79.   [76] *Id.*, p. 88.
[77] Arkhipov, in *Z.V.S.*, p. 92.   [78] *Id.*, pp. 93, 94.

the Party hierarchy in Russia. It is true that 'on July 19, 1919, the Central Committee (in Moscow) passed a special resolution ... by which Siberian Bolshevik underground organizations were required to establish the closest touch with Partisan forces'; and the Central Committee went on to urge Party workers with the Fifth Red Army to establish similar contact.[79] But such contact, up to the complete collapse of the White regime, was in fact never established. A Partisan participant has recorded that as late as October 'we could only get information about the Red Army from such Kolchak newspapers as came our way'.[80] It was not till this period that the first line crosser from Soviet-held territory made his way to Gromov's Partisans in the Altai.[81] And in spite of exhortations from Moscow, the Revolutionary Military Soviet of the Fifth Red Army remained sceptical. 'It was not yet clear', I. N. Smirnov records of the Partisans, 'what their attitude towards the Soviet Government was going to be to-morrow'.[82]

Party members like Yakovenko and Arkhipov did their best to counter Socialist Revolutionary tendencies. We have an order, signed by Arkhipov, expressing sharp displeasure at the retention in a number of villages in the Altai of the Zemstva set up under the Provisional Government.[83] (In the neighbouring Tomsk Province a peasant congress had voted two months previously, by a majority of 38 votes to 7 against the introduction of village soviets.)[84] It is certain that the S.R. element in the various Partisan movements became of less and less importance, and that the system of administration by soviets, always predominating, finally became almost universal in Partisan territory; and it is probable that the influence of the few Party members within the various movements was stronger in the autumn of 1919 that it had been in the spring.

However, the isolation of these Party members from the Party in Russia and the Party leadership in Moscow is a factor that must again be emphasized. The Bolshevism of these Siberian fighters was that of the winter of 1917-18, before hard physical necessity and repeated experience of human weakness had blunted or modified revolutionary idealism, or had established the fiat of exclusive Party dictatorship. In May 1918 there were still S.R.s and Mensheviks in the Central Executive Committee of the All-Russian Congress of Soviets. 'All power to the Soviets' had not, in Siberia in 1919, come to imply 'All

---

[79] Zobachev, in *Z.V.S.*, p. 36.
[80] Danilov, in *Z.V.S.*, p. 106.
[81] Gromov, in *Z.V.S.*, p. 68.
[82] Smirnov, in *Borba za Ural i Sibir*, p. 313.
[83] Document in *Z.V.S.*, p. 320.
[84] Kolosov, *op. cit.*, p. 32.

power to the Bolshevik Party machine'. The conception of freedom, the conception of the new Utopia held by the leaders, whether Bolshevik or not, was not incompatible with that held by the rank and file.

There is no statement of ultimate Partisan aims in what Partisan records have been preserved for us. The struggle is described as one for freedom, for deliverance from Kolchak tyranny, for the establishment of a new order, for soviets of peasants', soldiers', and workers' deputies. But no attempt is made to provide a blueprint for the future; or to define the future relationship of the Partisan administrations to an All-Russian Revolutionary government. Of interest is what these Partisan records do not contain. At the Stepnoi-Badzhei Peasant Congress in Section (xiv) there is no mention of Moscow, of the Soviet government or of the Bolshevik Party. The Red Army is referred to once, as 'brothers', doing, by implication, the same sort of job as the Partisans themselves were doing. There is no suggestion that the United Soviet of the Kansk, Krasnoiarsk and Achinsk Departments was a temporary or provisional body, or that it was due to be subordinated to any superior authority. It was obvious that the old ruling classes should be debarred from political activity; but the others, the working peasants, the workers and the 'working intellectuals', were to get together in their respective areas, freely elect their representatives and proceed to manage their own affairs.

As already stated, the Soviet authorities have been selective in their release of surviving Partisan records. We have only short extracts from *Sokha i Molot*, which for the last few months was the official organ of the Kravchenko-Shchetinkin command. We are told that this newspaper often showed anarchist tendencies, and paid not infrequent tributes to Bakunin.[85] For obvious reasons we are given no records of the movement led by Rogov and Novoselov which dominated a large area of the Tomsk province and which gave almost as much trouble to the Kolchak authorities as the movements described in these pages. But we may assume that there as elsewhere the basic Partisan aim was to secure for the villages a complete freedom from interference from the towns: and that there, as elsewhere, the approach of the Fifth Red Army was hailed as a guarantee for the perpetuation of this freedom. When in due course the last Kolchak forces were driven out and the Soviet regime started to consolidate its hold upon the villages as well as the towns there came the inevitable disillusionment and friction. And in

[85] Kolosov, *op. cit.*, p. 34.

the course of what Smirnov describes as the Siberian 'Makh-novshchina'[86] both Rogov and Novoselov were killed fighting against the Bolsheviks. The Party leadership in Moscow was well aware that the Partisan movements constituted a potential threat both to centralized administration and to the Party leadership's autocracy, and this was clearly expressed in Trotsky's report to the Seventh Congress of Soviets in December 1919.[87]

(xviii)

Yakovenko's memoirs give a vivid little account of the end of the Civil War in his part of Siberia.[88] December saw the complete collapse of the Whites. White garrisons mutinied and their officers were killed or captured. (We learn that of the fifteen officers with the battalion at Mokrashino two were forwarded alive to Partisan headquarters and the other thirteen executed on the spot as 'scoundrels'.) After Kolchak's convoy of trains had passed through Kansk the town lapsed into chaos and a joint delegation from the mutinied White garrison, the Zemstvo and the Co-operatives appealed to the Taseevo head-quarters as the one stable authority in the neighbourhood. Yakovenko and his colleagues in the Military Soviet of the Northern Kansk Front agreed to take over the town on con-dition that they had complete control. The Czechs were still guarding the railway line and a Czech force held the station. Partisans and Czechs agreed to leave each other alone. In early January the last White Army under General Kappel arrived along the road from the west. After some sharp fighting the Whites by-passed the town and proceeded eastwards. Shortly afterwards the Fifth Red Army approached, and the officer commanding the advance guard (contrary to the policy of his own superiors) sent a message to Yakovenko instructing him to attack the Czechs. As this would have meant damaging the railway Yakovenko stalled: he waited till the Czechs departed and attacked their last echelon some forty miles to the east. Then the Red Army arrived in Kansk and took over. Some of the Partisans were incorporated in the regular forces, the rest were demobilized and sent home. Yakovenko himself and some of his collaborators took on responsible positions in the new Soviet administration. The last available mention of him is his retirement on grounds of ill health in 1926. It is very possible

---

[86] Smirnov, in *Borba za Ural i Sibir*, p. 313.
[87] Trotsky, *Nashe Voennoe Stroitelstvo, Nashi Fronty* (Moscow, 1919).
[88] Yakovenko, *op. cit.*, pp. 45, 46.

that he was a victim of one of the great purges of the thirties.

Details of the closing stages of other Partisan groups have been left by a member of the commission set up by the Fifth Red Army for the final regulation of Partisan affairs.[89] The first sight the commission had of the movement, on their journey to the Altai, was of lines of peasant carts going home across the steppe, loaded with loot from the town of Kamen. The Partisan rank and file, conceiving their struggle to be a war of the villages against the towns, were making sure of the spoils of victory.[90] Kamen itself was in complete disorder. What little remained to loot was being looted. No guards were posted, not even at Partisan headquarters. Gromov, the Officer Commanding, was drunk and, though some White detachments were reported to be in the neighbourhood, no Partisan authority could be persuaded to take steps to locate and attack them. There was similar chaos in Barnaul, with threats of mutiny by the rank and file following a quarrel with the staff over the distribution of the contents of a liquor store. In Semipalatinsk (where there had been a massacre of local Cossacks) Kozyr, the Partisan Commandant, informed the commission that 'he could not, for the moment, define his attitude to the Soviet authorities because he did not know how the Soviet authorities would behave in the future.'[91]

The Commission's task was a difficult one. Resistance to an outside authority had become part of Partisan mentality. They elected their own commanders, and, in any case, 'Soviets come from peasants, not from commanders'. In the end, and helped by the prestige of the Red Army, the Commission's skill and pertinacity were rewarded. Manageable detachments of suitable volunteers were sent off to be enrolled in the regular Red Army. The remaining Partisans were disarmed, more or less. Some of the leaders, including Gromov, Arkhipov and the Commander in Chief Mamontov went off west to conduct guerilla operations against Wrangel.[92]

Kravchenko and Shchetinkin had a larger popular appeal than any of the other Partisan leaders: their names had become a legend well outside the area of their operations. It was therefore decided, as has already been mentioned, to convert their

[89] V. Eltsin, in *B. za U. i S.*, pp. 267-75.

[90] On the capture of Kuznetsk by Rogov and Novoselov this anti-town hostility brought about a pogrom of the professional classes—Kolosov, *op. cit.*, p. 30.

[91] Eltsin, in *B. za U. i S.*, p. 274.

[92] Arkhipov in *Z.V.S.*, p. 97. After an adventurous campaign in south-west Russia, Mamontov came back to his farm in the Altai. He took no part of any kind in the peasant unrest of 1920. He was killed by 'kulaks' early in 1922—Note by Yarolavski in *Prol. Rev.*, No. 6 (1922), pp. 224-5.

force into a regular division of the Red Army with headquarters at Achinsk.[93] Kravchenko became the titular divisional commander; but there was a political staff, composed of officers seconded from the Fifth Red Army with wide powers of control and with the special task of enforcing regular army discipline. There was friction from the start. Partisan officers and men became restive and wanted the old order back again. The new regulations were ignored or evaded. Kravchenko made no effort to co-operate with the political staff, and took to drink. He foresaw that a show-down was coming, and attempted to make a bolt to Minusinsk. He was caught and arrested. The Red Army authorities appealed to Shchetinkin to come to headquarters and exert his influence to prevent a mutiny. But his men at first refused to let Shchetinkin proceed; they were convinced that if he did he would be arrested. In the end, however, he did come into Achinsk and, after much argument, the Partisans were persuaded to hand in their arms and disperse. But one of Kravchenko's brigades had to be disarmed by force.

In the relatively tolerant atmosphere of 1920 Kravchenko was given the chance to rehabilitate himself. Like other Partisan leaders he was sent westwards and took part in the Polish war. Then he came back to Siberia and was employed in the Agricultural Directorate (Gubzemupravlenie) of the Yenisei province. He died in 1924, leaving an uncompleted manuscript memoir which is now in the archives at Novosibirsk.[94]

Shchetinkin, after the dispersal of the Peasant Army, served for a time at Achinsk under the Military Revolutionary Soviet of the Fifth Red Army. Then he went to south-west Russia and commanded first a battalion and then a regiment against Wrangel. Subsequently he was appointed, at the instance of the Far Eastern Secretariat of the Comintern, to command the Red forces against Ungern-Sternberg. After Ungern's defeat and capture in August 1921 he went to Moscow to report and was awarded the order of the Red Banner. In 1923 he was made Chief of Staff of the G.P.U. Siberian Frontier Troops with headquarters at Novosibirsk; and his wife who had been with him on the long trek from Krasnovka to Stepnoi-Badzhei, and on the far longer one down to Tanu-Tuva and back, was at last able for a few years to enjoy a settled home.[95] In the late summer of 1927 the Mongolian People's Government invited Shchetinkin to Urga (Ulan Bator) to be instructor to their new

[93] Eltsin, in *B. za U. i S.*, pp. 275-9.
[94] Shchetinkin, *op. cit.*, Appendix, p. 68.
[95] Vassa Shchetinkin, in *Z.V.S.*, p. 197.

Military Security Service. He died a few days after his arrival there. His widow maintains that he was 'murdered by Japanese agents'. A later authority ascribes his death to heart failure. His body was brought back to Novosibirsk for a state funeral.[96]

[96] Shchetinkin, *op. cit.*, Foreword by Vegman, pp. 12, 13.

ECONOMICS IN THE U.S.S.R.

By Alec Nove

WHAT are the functions of economics, and of economists in the U.S.S.R.? This is a subject of some interest, bearing not only on the nature of the Soviet regime, but also on the more general question of the role of economics in a planned society. It is a topical problem, too, because changes are taking place in the Soviet view of what economists should do.

The term 'economist' in Russia is used loosely to cover quite junior employees, on enterprise level, engaged on costing and other semi-accountancy duties, and paid a salary considerably below that of an averagely skilled factory worker. Such 'economists' are extremely numerous, but are not the subject of the present paper, which is concerned with academic activity, and with the application of economic analysis to central planning and policy.

There is no shortage of academic economists. In the academic year 1953-4 there were 286 departments of economics in institutions of university status. Many of these institutions are of a technically specialized character, under various economic ministries—for example the Moscow Machine-building Institute possesses a department of economics. The universities and colleges directly administered by the Ministry of Higher Education have 191 economics departments, in which there is a teaching staff of 2,394, including 46 professors.[1] At the head of the profession, there is the Economics Institute of the Academy of Sciences of the U.S.S.R., responsible for the general supervision of doctrine and publication; the Institute itself has a research staff, and publishes monographs on various subjects. It edits the principal specialist periodical, the monthly *Voprosy Ekonomiki* (Questions of Economics), and at times organizes all-union conferences to discuss questions of current importance.

Various government departments employ senior economists. The top planning agency, 'Gosplan' (now split into two) is naturally outstanding among such departments; it runs train-

[1] Dyachenko, in *Voprosy Ekonomiki*, No. 10/1955 (hereinafter referred to as Dyachenko).

ing courses, undertakes research and publishes a bi-monthly organ devoted mainly to economic subjects, *Planovoe Khozaistvo*. There exist also trade and finance research institutes, under the respective ministries. The Central Statistical Office (C.S.O.) attached to the Council of Ministers is naturally closely concerned with economic problems; it has its own research activities and a bi-monthly organ, *Vestnik Statistiki*. The C.S.O. employs numerous economists both in Moscow and in its local offices, as does the state banking system. Finally, the central organization of the Communist party must have an important economics department, although little is known of its size and functions.

The teaching of economics in the U.S.S.R. is handicapped by being so close to the heart of Marxism. For reasons too complex to discuss here, there has arisen a tradition of extremely rigid, 'biblical' interpretation of the 'classics of Marxism-Leninism'. This affects economists more than most other specialists for an obvious reason: whereas physicists or biologists have run into difficulties from time to time in reconciling their ideas with Marxist orthodoxy, neither Marx nor Engels actually wrote a text-book of physics or biology, and so there are wide areas of research in which the Soviet scientist need have little fear of colliding with Marxian dogma. Unfortunately for the economics profession, Marx did write a systematic treatise on economics, and this limits the room for manoeuvring within the area of permissible orthodoxy. Marx, of course, wrote about the 'capitalism' of his day. Whatever the truth of his analysis, it is unlikely to apply without serious amendment to western society seventy years after his death; even less appropriate can his teaching be to the analysis of Soviet conditions. In the atmosphere of the Stalin era, this proved a particularly severe handicap to Soviet economists. It may be that Marxist analytical methods, applied undogmatically in the course of a serious assessment of reality, can yield good results. This view is not contradicted by Soviet experience, since such analyses have hardly ever been attempted, or, if attempted, have not been published. Economists were especially limited in their scope, because, firstly, economic researches on 'Soviet' questions bear directly on *policy*, i.e. in the Soviet context on politics; secondly, any original work on the economies of the 'capitalist' countries was rendered impossible by the insistence on over-simplification, a black-and-white approach, a 'militant' attitude. Nor could any attempt at a historical description of Soviet economic development depart from the official view of events, laid down all too clearly in the authoritative *Short History of the Communist Party of the U.S.S.R.*

Yet it is only right to add that, while professional economists had little function and less influence, there is a sense in which economic theory played a quite vital determining role in the formulation of basic policy. Marx's economics was intimately linked with his ideas about the revolutionary transformation of society, and the minds of the Communist leadership has been impregnated with these ideas. It would take us far beyond the scope of this paper to discuss the relative importance of Marxian theory in the shaping of Soviet policies, but no one doubts that Russia has in fact been transformed in ways profoundly influenced by Marx's economic analyses. One might say that the leaders have been so busy changing Russia, and so intent on harnessing all theoretical and practical activity for this purpose, that there has been little room for the views of professional economists or for the development of economic theory on ordinary, prosaic lines. Thus, if one is engaged in an all-out battle to destroy peasant individualism, one's ears are scarcely likely to be tuned to arguments about costs per unit or relative efficiency in agriculture. Economic reality is then seen in terms of struggle, and economic calculation as *we* know it becomes relatively insignificant. Of course, ordinary economic problems do not disappear, but they do find themselves submerged. They re-emerge in due course, as we shall see, and it can be argued that this re-emergence was delayed by the peculiarly tight strait-jacket imposed on all intellectual life in the last half of Stalin's 'reign'.

What then is an economics course in a Soviet university? What research can an economist carry out under such conditions?

A university course, from the available evidence, deals with the subject under three heads: first, basic theory; second, a survey of 'capitalist' development; thirdly, the economy of the U.S.S.R.

The theoretical basis consists of a fairly detailed study of the Marxist formulations, with discussions on the theory of value, exploitation, the recurrence of crises, the circulation of capital, and the rest. The so-called 'classical' economists—Adam Smith and Ricardo in particular—are treated sympathetically; they at least sought to deal with economic developments in their wider contexts, to analyse reality. This is contrasted with the 'vulgar economists', whose father is generally stated to be J.-B. Say, and who reach their apogee with the development of the marginal utility theory. They are guilty of mistaking surface symptoms for reality, they are crude apologists for capitalism, and so on. This presentation has shown no noticeable development since Marx's death, and indeed the 'vulgar' are commonly assailed in the relevant books with quotations from Marx and Engels.

The treatment of twentieth-century 'capitalist' development tends to be much cruder. It is generally prefaced by an analysis of Lenin's theory of Imperialism, and since 1952 also by Stalin's views about warlike robber-exploitation by monopolists striving for maximum profits. These ideas, in conjunction with the grimmest of Marx's assaults on the capitalism of his day, have formed the basis of the attack on Western economics and Western economists. The crudity of this kind of exposition almost passes belief. The following example is taken from the authoritative economics textbook published in 1954 (though the tone is more typical of the period immediately preceding Stalin's death, when the book was being written):

The general law of capitalist accumulation is the concrete expression of the functioning of the basic economic law of capitalism—the law of surplus value. The striving after surplus value leads to the concentration of riches in the exploiting classes, and the growth of unemployment, poverty and exploitation among the propertyless masses.

With the development of capitalism, there occurs the relative and absolute pauperization of the proletariat. . . .

The *absolute pauperization* of the proletariat consists in a direct reduction in living standards.

'The worker becomes poorer in absolute terms, i.e. he becomes more impoverished, must live under worse conditions, eat less well, often go hungry, shelter in cellar and attics.' . . . (Lenin)

With the aim of whitewashing reality, bourgeois economics seeks to deny the absolute pauperization of the proletariat. However, the facts show that the standard of living of the workers under capitalism falls lower and lower. This may be seen in a number of ways.

The absolute pauperization of the proletariat shows itself in falling real wages. As has already been said, consequent upon systematic price increases, rises in rents, increases in taxes, real wages of the workers fall continuously. In the twentieth century, the real wages of the workers in England, U.S.A., France, Italy and other capitalist countries stand at a lower level than in the middle of the nineteenth century.

The absolute pauperization of the masses shows itself in the increase in the magnitude and duration of unemployment.

The absolute pauperization of the masses shows itself in the limitless rise in the intensity of, and the worsening of the conditions of labour; the worker rapidly deteriorates, loses his ability to work, becomes an invalid. Consequent upon the increased labour intensity, and the absence of measures for labour protection, there is an enormous increase in accidents and injuries in factories.

. . . The absolute pauperization of the masses shows itself in a sharp deterioration in the diet and living conditions of the toilers causing ill-health, a higher death rate, reduced expectation of life of the working population. . . . In connection with the increased pauperization of the toilers, the birth-rate has fallen as follows, from the 1870s to the 1930s, per thousand: in England, from 36 to 15, in Germany, from 39 to 19, in France, from 26 to 15. (pp. 142-4)

The textbook is the joint work of nine professors, under the auspices of the Institute of Economics of the Academy of Sciences. Printed in five million copies, it is, thus far, the only available book published in the last twenty-five years which treats economics systematically. No direct criticism of its approach to the 'bourgeois' world has yet appeared, though an appeal for more serious and less dogmatic study of the Western world, to be cited later, may be interpreted as adverse comment.

The treatment of Western economists as apologists for monopoly profiteers and warmongers was equally crude.

The economists were prisoners of the compulsory militant posture imposed on all Soviet intellectuals in their public pronouncements on the Western world. This by no means excluded a quite considerable knowledge of real developments; there were detailed studies on such subjects as the role of gold in the South African balance of payments and a serious analysis of some of Keynes' theories, but one learns of such things indirectly, by reference to doctorate theses, or by the undercurrent of scholarship discernible even in the course of a crude denunciation of Keynes the 'warmonger'.[2]

In the years following the war, an attempt was indeed made to treat Western problems more subtly, to differentiate between different countries, and to consider the effects on traditional

[2] For example, in the otherwise deplorable book by Blyumin, *Kritika Soveremennoi Burzhuaznoi Ekonomiki Angliii* (Critique of Contemporary bourgeois English economics), 1953.

'capitalism' of wartime and postwar developments. (At this period, Keynes' *General Theory* was translated and published in Russia.) This manifested itself particularly in the Institute of World Economy and World Politics, headed by the well-known Hungarian economist, Varga. The more enlightened trend culminated in the publication, in 1947, of Varga's book, *Changes in the capitalist economy following the second world war*. The book and its tendencies were shortly afterwards condemned, in May 1947, and the Institute dissolved. The author admitted his errors, while retaining a reduced but respected position among Soviet economists. Others learned their lesson, and crude caricatures of the west became the rule. There was no significant change in this during the first two years after Stalin's death, though much was happening in other spheres of learning.

It would be understandable if, while unimaginatively following Marxist-Leninist orthodoxy in the treatment of the 'hostile' West, Soviet economists concentrated on devising theories which were relevant to their own economic structure. Unfortunately, this was not the case.

This failure, as we shall see, is now openly admitted. Western critics are sometimes apt to take the view that failure was inevitable because economics as such has little meaning in a planned, centralized society. This view is, surely, mistaken. The following may be cited as examples of essentially economic problems, highly relevant to the theory and practice of the Soviet state, on which economists should have something to say:

(*a*) What principles should guide one in measuring the relative economic advantages of alternative lines of investment?

(*b*) What should be the role of prices under the Soviet system? Should prices of producers' goods reflect relative scarcities? If not, by what means should the use of scarce materials be discouraged? How far should prices be a guide towards desirable lines of production, and should managers be given a range of choice which is related to price-levels?

(*c*) The collective farms are under an obligation to meet delivery quotas at low prices. What are the economic consequences of this? Are price relativities rational? If not, what ought they to be to achieve the desired fiscal results while stimulating output? What basic principles are involved? How should these be related to regional specialization on given products?

(*d*) How can one measure costs and productivity in agriculture, in the Soviet institutional setting? What is the 'value' of, say, a ton of wheat, and how can one set about determining it?

(*e*) Wages are unequal, because of the need to provide incentives and to reward skill and energy. What theory of wages is appropriate to the U.S.S.R.?

(*f*) On what basis should the state plan the relationship between the output of producers' goods and consumers' goods? What are the consequences of given changes in, and within, these categories on the rate of growth of the economy?

(*g*) What relevance, if any, and what practical significance as a guide to action, has the theory of value to the Soviet economy?

The list could be prolonged.

It would be both unfair and inaccurate to state that none of these problems received attention. It is necessary to distinguish between the *general theoretical* field, where practically nothing was done, and some important specialized debates, though there was relatively little to report even there.

No general textbook of economics was published in the U.S.S.R. between 1930 and 1954. This in itself shows the difficulty encountered in devising any theory adequate to explain Soviet reality in a systematic way. University courses and occasional general expositions in articles tended to take the following road: firstly, a general theory of national income, closely derived from Marx, was developed and applied to the Soviet economy; this led to difficulties over such questions as the dividing line between productive and unproductive labour, but nevertheless coped fairly adequately with the conceptual problem involved.[3] Secondly, there was generally a long economic account of Soviet economic institutions and their normal (somewhat idealized) functioning. Thus, the student was told about the budget, profit-and-loss accounting in state enterprises, the various categories of prices, the rules by which wages should be determined, the various types of farms, and so on. Many important subjects were touched upon, but without grappling with the real problems. This is particularly evident in the economics textbook published in 1954, following upon long discussions in high academic circles, in which Stalin took part in 1951-2. This book's approach to potentially controversial matters might be characterized as follows: the state does what is right, what is right is what the state does. Objective economic laws, if any are formulated, are always obeyed by the state, indeed, it becomes all but a law that they *are* observed. Several examples can be used to demonstrate this fact: thus,

[3] On this question, see P. Studenski in *Studies in Income and Wealth*, Vol. VIII (1946), and also Nove in *Soviet Studies* (Glasgow, January, 1955).

the economics textbook and other texts declare that there exists the 'law of planned-proportionate-development of the economy' and that the necessary proportions are, in accordance with this law, established by the state. It is true that Stalin, in his last work, stated that it could not be *assumed* that the planners have been successful in obeying the law, but other authors generally leave out this qualification; the textbook does indeed mention it, but only in the sense that planning errors can lead to a shortage of this or that material. The basic *direction* of economic policy seems to be a law unto itself, correct by definition.

On a similar level is the statement that the Soviet state aims at maximizing the satisfaction of the consumer; this, too, is raised to the dignity of an economic 'law'. The meaning of the term 'law' in such a context is far from clear, unless it is intended to aver that *any given level of consumption decided upon by the state* is the maximum possible at the given stage of economic development. Another example concerns wages: there is ample evidence from specialized journals that the actual wages structure is greatly influenced by the supply-and-demand for labour in conditions of over-full employment, and that this has greatly distorted the formal structure; much of this has now been admitted by the prime minister,[4] and a committee has been set up to devise a more effective wages structure. Yet neither these realities, nor the underlying economic forces, have been analysed in any serious way, unless one excepts a few references to occasional departures from the letter of the regulations. A Soviet professor has at long last written, and no wonder, that the textbook 'cannot satisfy the need for a profound study of economics in universities. . . . A number of economic categories of Socialism are presented in the form of assertions (*deklarativno*).'[5] Just so.

The failure was most complete in agriculture, as has now been admitted in a whole series of articles[6]: no work had been done on how to measure productivity, no methodology of determining costs of production had been devised, the *rationale* of the farm price system had been almost entirely neglected. Economists merely repeated current policy slogans, illustrating them with detailed studies designed for the purpose, criticizing whatever had already been attacked by the party leaders.

The role of the law of value in Soviet conditions was a most

[4] Bulganin's speech, reported in *Pravda*, July 17, 1955.
[5] Dyachenko, p. 3.
[6] For example, in *Voprosy Ekonomiki*, Nos. 7 and 9/1955; *Sotsialisticheskoe Selskoe Khozaistvo*, No. 4/1955; etc. The subject is analysed in some detail by the writer in *Soviet Studies* (January, 1956).

intractable theoretical problem. In the early thirties, extreme views were common, to the effect that the law of value, indeed all economic laws, were henceforth non-existent for the U.S.S.R. By the end of the decade, economic laws became respectable again, and the doctrine was developed that 'the law of value in transformed guise' exists in, and is consciously used by, the Soviet state. In 1952 Stalin attacked this view, which he may well have himself formulated earlier,[7] in his *Economic Problems of Socialism*; one cannot, he claimed, 'transform' a law; the law of value applies to exchanges between the state and non-state (especially collective-peasant) sectors of the economy, and does not in essence apply to transactions *within* the state sector, such as the delivery of steel from one enterprise to another. This remains the official doctrine, and its constant repetition is still a substitute for considering a much more vital problem: how far value and prices do—or ought to—influence the actual behaviour of Soviet enterprises, farms and citizens. Stalin's formulation is in any event unsatisfactory, since it provides no *criterion* by which to identify 'values'. It was no accident that, in his own last work, he was forced to use *world* price relationships between wheat and cotton to show that this relationship had gone awry in the U.S.S.R.

In some specialized directions, economists were rather more active. For many years, there has been a discussion in the specialized press on measuring the returns from alternative lines of investment. (This discussion was confined to the important but limited field of comparing the profitabilities of different variants of the same project, e.g. a steam or electric railway. No one in the U.S.S.R. would suggest that, because shoes are more profitable than excavators, a shoe factory should have priority.) A leading part in these discussions was played by an able transport economist, Dr Khachaturov. The problem was complicated by the fact that a rate of interest, real or notional, is hard to fit into the Soviet theoretical pattern, but a lively if inconclusive debate occurred; a summary of this is available in English.[8] Other writers generally confined themselves to description, with occasional cautious criticism. For example, one can deduce from a book on the price system[9] that

[7] The formulation about a law of value in transformed form appeared in an unsigned article in a weighty party-theoretical organ, *Pod znamenem Marksizma*, in 1943, and has been attributed to Stalin personally.

[8] *Soviet Studies*, Vol. VI, p. 201. See also *id.* Vol. I, pp. 119, 356, Vol. II, p. 317, Vol. IV, p. 340, where some earlier discussions are wholly or partially translated.

[9] Maisenberg: *Tseno-obrazovanie v narodnom khozaistve S.S.S.R.* (Price formation in the U.S.S.R. economy) (1953).

economists and planners probably have a professional preference for a rationally interconnected pattern of prices.

In the period 1946-8, in which the appearance of Varga's book was already noted, there was for a time a relatively freer atmosphere, when were published some worthwhile works by Professors Rothstein and Notkin, among some others.[10] A conference of economists in 1948 heard criticism of the timidity of the profession, but further development was stifled by the general intellectual atmosphere of Stalin's last years. The condemnation of Voznesenski's book on the war economy in 1949, and the disappearance of its author, did nothing to encourage boldness in the profession, especially as the bulk of its members had greeted the book with a chorus of praise. But the picture as a whole, until Stalin's death, was, and to a large extent still is, singularly bleak.

Some readers may regard this analysis as too critical, or unfair to the Soviet economics profession. However, the director of the Institute of Economics of the Academy of Sciences, Professor Dyachenko, has had some very harsh things to say on this same subject in the October (No. 10/1955) issue of *Voprosy Ekonomiki*. He confirms, most frankly, that original work was conspicuous by its absence, and that the 'authorities' were endlessly and uncritically cited. 'Until recently, dogmatism and the "biblical" approach (*nachyotnichetsvo*) showed themselves most openly in "quotationism". Instead of profound independent economic researches, many authors busied themselves with collecting and commenting upon quotations. Facts were selected and cited only for confirming and illustrating the assertions contained in the quotations. Matters went so far that the number of quotations was regarded as the measure of an author's "erudition". An economist who found a quotation which had not been used many times in other economists' works considered himself a creative scholar, an original thinker, so to speak. In arguments, between economists, the main role was played, once again, by quotations. After vigorous criticism of dogmatism and the "biblical" approach in the party press, quotations diminished, but often only on the surface. Quotations lost their quotation marks, were amended editorially, but the real situation remained unchanged.' The professor admits that 'the selection of new illustrations to accepted principles is

---

[10] A. Rothstein, *Promyshlennaya Statistika*, Vol. III (1947; first two volumes published before the war), and A. I. Notkin, *Ocherki teorii sotsialisticheskovo vosproizvodstva* (1948). The state of affairs at this period was well described by A. Zamberman in *Review of Economic Studies* (1949-50), Nos. 40-41.

necessary, especially in educational and propaganda work, but this does not determine the content of genuine research.' Little research is in fact carried out by academic staffs. 'The study of key questions of political economy is the most backward sector. For many years there has not been a single worth-while general theoretical work.' Most doctoral dissertations follow narrow, theoretically insignificant lines, such as 'The importance of avoiding waste, vital lever for raising the level of the paper industry', or 'The organization of labour and production' in one collective farm (his example). All this is not due to any lack of unresolved problems; on the contrary 'these are endless'. 'Every work since the economic discussion of 1951 [i.e. Stalin's pronouncement, published the next year] mentions the objective character of economic laws under socialism, yet not a single work has been published which thoroughly examines in what the objective character of such laws finds expression, how the requirements of any of these laws are put into effect, how breaches of these laws can be identified.' Professor Dyachenko lists other gaping voids in economic research: proportions and interconnections of various branches of the economy, problems of prices, technical progress and so on. Agricultural economists 'as a rule confined themselves to repeating and commenting on decisions arrived at by the party and government, with not a few errors and distortions.'

He also criticizes crude oversimplification in analysing modern capitalism, denial of technical and scientific progress in the West. 'The study of the latest developments of contemporary capitalism is extremely defective.' It is also necessary to 'end the situation in which certain scholars, due to their ignorance, or to some other cause, [*sic*!] label all economists in capitalist countries who are non-Marxist-Leninists as reactionaries.' There is even no serious study of Marxian economics; apart from an unfinished work by a deceased specialist, the history of Marxian thought 'is not studied at the Institute of Economics of the Academy, or, it seems, in other institutes and universities.'

All this is indeed true, and no student of Soviet economics can do other than deplore the appallingly low general-theoretical standard; one can but hope that this vigorous public attack by a leader of the profession is a sign that better times are coming.

There were signs of progress in some sectors of economic study after Stalin's death. During 1954 some original contributions, by lesser-known economists, began to be printed in specialized periodicals. These questioned or criticized various concepts. For instance, the official definition of 'productive' activity was attacked, and the failings of agricultural statistics exposed with some frankness.[11] More important, the Economics Institute of the Academy organized a discussion, early in 1954, on the relative rates of increase in the output of producers' goods and consumers' goods, at a time when the Malenkov government was stressing the accelerated growth of consumers' goods production. The less thoughtful economists promptly produced formulations reflecting this new policy. They did this in a most naive way, showing no sign of having studied the effect of a change in composition of industrial output on the pattern and rate of growth of the economy. One economist, it is true, advanced a more sophisticated argument, which readers of Colin Clark's work will recognize: that the relative *cost* of investment goods is showing a tendency to fall, and that therefore by implication the proportion of national income devoted to investment could also fall in terms of current prices. This argument, along with the cruder formulations, was denounced in January 1955, when the priority of producers' goods over consumers' goods was vigorously reasserted by the Party. The erring economists were criticized in a series of articles in theoretical journals, and the Institute of Economics had to apologize for having printed offending articles in *Voprosy Ekonomiki* and for permitting the discussion to take the course which it followed.[12]

However, before this counter-attack, a more original approach to the question of the balance of the economy was made by Professor Strumilin,[13] one of the older generation of economists, which was not included in the above criticisms and is being further developed. Strumilin argued that it is necessary to study the effect of varying the output of different categories of goods on future rates of growth of various sectors, and attempted a new approach to the interconnection of the different elements in the economy, even daring to imply that one of Marx's formulations was in need of revision. Strumilin's detailed argument, which this is not the place to examine, suffers from some serious shortcomings, but represents a (by Soviet standards) bold attempt to grapple with a problem ignored by his colleagues.

[11] For example, Bor in *Voprosy Ekonomiki*, No. 10/1954.

[12] Self-critical articles appeared in *Voprosy Ekonomiki*, No. 1/1955; *Finansy S.S.S.R.*, No. 2/1955, etc.

[13] *Voprosy Ekonomiki*, No. 11/1954 and *Vestnik Statistiki* No. 5/1954. See also A. Gabor in *Yorkshire Bulletin of Economics and Social Research . . .*, M. Dobb, in *Soviet Studies*, July 1955, and Gabor's criticism of Dobb in the issue of October 1955.

In recent months, the 'thaw' has extended most of all to the field of agricultural economics, where quite fundamental questions of price pattern, costs and productivity have come into the area of permissible discussion.[14] Vital problems connected with regional specialization of agriculture have been discussed in quite stimulating language by Academician Nemchinov.[15] Khachaturov has raised some basic questions affecting both the economic analysis of transport and state price and construction policy.[16] The question of depreciation and obsolescence has been reopened, and some original articles have appeared, which no longer assume that obsolescence is a meaningless category in the U.S.S.R.[17] Dyachenko has urged bolder studies of the price pattern, the stimulation of technical efficiency, wages, the practical significance of the theory of value and other such matters. The status and role of economists have been raised by the recent decisions to create new economics institutes as follows: Agricultural economics, Planning (within Gosplan), Labour and wages (attached to the ministerial committee dealing with these problems), Location of Industry and regionalization, and finally, (within the Institute of Economics of the Academy of Sciences) Contemporary capitalism.

All this is, of course, an encouraging change from the grim intellectual desert of the late-Stalin epoch. However, the improvement is a limited one. The limitations can probably best be understood by reference to the purpose of the 'thaw' from the Party's point of view. There is little doubt that the Party leadership had been watching the performance of the economists with increasing impatience, and this can readily be understood; of what use to any government are 'economists' who equate ultimate wisdom with *any* policy which the government may devise? Facing many problems, Stalin's successors turn to economists for advice, and are justifiably irritated at the response. Angry criticism of the poor performance of the profession appeared, for example, in the Party's theoretical organ *Kommunist*.[18] No doubt much can be explained by the fact that, at the present stage of Soviet economic development, questions concerned with the most efficient use of limited resources of labour and materials—*economic* problems—urgently require solution, in a political setting no longer dominated by an absolute dictator. The old servility and timidity can serve no useful purpose, and so the economists are being cajoled and

---

[14] For example, see sources cited in footnote 6.
[15] *Planovoe Khozaistvo*, No. 4/1955.   [16] *Voprosy Ekonomiki*, No. 9/1955.
[17] For instance, Konson in *Vestnik Statistiki*, No. 5/1955.   [18] No. 7/1955.

prodded to get up off their knees. From sheer force of habit, and recalling the unsatisfactory careers of the bolder spirits of the profession, some of them find an upright posture an unfamiliar strain. Dyachenko rightly attacks his colleagues' 'fear of discussing controversial questions'.

But—and in Soviet affairs there always is a 'but'—the state is evidently not willing to grant economists freedom of research or publication, as we understand these things. The great and welcome extension of the area of intellectual activity by economists should not blind one to this fact. Even Dyachenko himself follows his clarion call for boldness with a denunciation of those who, 'through apathy and an attitude of compromise' provided a 'platform for the woeful economists who revised one of the basic principles of Marxism-Leninism, concerning the priority of growth of producers' goods. . . .' Views regarded as unorthodox or erroneous, then, have *no* right of expression, save within certain limits. These limits, judging from the discussions so far printed, would seem to be as follows: a range of possible suggestions and formulations is invited, which would help the Party and government to devise better methods of carrying out their basic economic policies, as these are from time to time announced. This does afford a considerable area for independent thought. For example, a quite wide range of theories and practical suggestions would fall within the general lines of the present agricultural and industrial policies. In the years of 'frost' the economists had virtually no constructive professional role in devising solutions to economic problems, while theoretical work practically lapsed. Their present role, despite its limitations, does give them the opportunity to show that, despite the bleak, blank years, they can contribute positively to knowledge, and to the improvement of the institutional and price structures of the Soviet economy.

ADDENDUM

Since the above was written, there have been further signs of the adoption of a less negative attitude to the West and to Western economists. This is no doubt closely connected with the repeated requests to study advanced Western technique, a task unlikely to be encouraged by a theory which declares the West to be in an advanced state of decomposition. A most interesting example of the extent and limitations of the new 'line' is provided by the second edition of the economics textbook, which has just reached this country. There are a number of amendments, and the most relevant one for our present purpose is the inclusion of a new section, 'The basic economic task', which is that of eventually outstripping the United States in technique and productivity. Consequently, some of the more absurd statements about the collapse of capitalism are omitted, or left in a vague future tense. However, all the passages quoted in the text of the present paper have been retained, with the one exception of the statement about the fall in birth rates since 1870 being connected with the impoverishment of the masses. It is also no longer asserted that wages in the U.K. are 20% below pre-war (p. 292, first edition); they are just 'lower' (p. 300, second edition). A new section now singles out, and takes a rather patronizing attitude to 'petty-bourgeois economists' in the West, who are against American imperialism and criticize monopoly-capitalism (p. 317), but no names are mentioned.

Keynes is criticized in equally harsh terms in both editions, but instead of asserting that his 'theory is utterly baseless and deeply reactionary' (p. 307, first edition), it is now just 'baseless' (p. 315, second edition). Right wing labour leaders are no longer 'agents of the imperialist bourgeoisie in the labour movement' (p. 317, first edition), but are still vigorously assailed. The substance of the old line has been retained, but some epithets are now omitted, which, one supposes, is progress. The second edition was sent to the printers at about the same time as Dyachenko's article appeared, i.e. in October 1955, and it may or may not represent the present (January) view held on how to analyse Western countries.

So far as the analysis of the Soviet economy is concerned, the new edition only marginally differs from the old.

THE IDEOLOGICAL FUNCTIONARY

By Wolfgang Leonhard

IT is widely believed in the West that the regime in the U.S.S.R. and the East Bloc countries is solely based on terror and force: only an insignificant section of the population are held to be Stalinist fanatics, while the overwhelming majority are opponents or neutrals.

This conception seems, however, to ignore the real problems. Naturally there is an unbelievably complex apparatus of terror and repression, but this alone can by no means explain the fact that those who sometimes criticize certain aspects or policies of the system are sincere and firmly convinced Stalinists. They are filled with the Stalinist faith and ready to work, to hunger, and even to die for the system.

An important question must therefore be: How and by what means has Stalinism succeeded in building up a completely loyal class of functionaries through which it has been able to influence a large portion of the population—in particular the younger generation?

The Significance of Educational Training

In my opinion the answer lies in the Party education and training which plays a far greater role than is generally assumed in the West, and which is so thorough that it guarantees a completely independent execution of the Party line by each functionary.

The great importance attached to Party schooling is shown by the two following examples:

Early in June 1945 the exiled leadership of the K.P.D. (including Wilhelm Pieck and Fred Oelssner) arrived in Berlin from Moscow. They brought with them not only explicit directives for the future political development of Germany but also a directive that after the re-establishment of the Communist Party in Germany a programme of obligatory schooling (one evening each week) should be instituted for all members of the Party. Within two days of his arrival Fred Oelssner had dictated the first instruction pamphlet for the members of the as yet non-existent K.P.D. The first pamphlet appeared as early as July 1945 and with so precise a content as to be astonishing in view of the situation at that period. Long before the Potsdam Conference, at a time when the Western occupation authorities were by no means decided about their political measures in Germany, hundreds of thousands of Party members were already being politically schooled in the Soviet zone. The first boarding-schools of the Party, with four-week courses, had been set up by the autumn of 1945.

A second example: As we know, the S.E.D. suffered a crushing defeat in the Berlin elections on October 20, 1946. Prior to the elections the inner circle of the S.E.D. had expected the S.E.D. to emerge as the strongest party in Germany; in the event the Party received only 19·8% of the votes and dropped to third place. The opponents of the S.E.D. celebrated their victory without realizing that the S.E.D. leadership had taken far-reaching steps immediately following the election defeat. Two days after the election Otto Grotewohl visited the Party's education section and said: 'The elections showed that the frontal attack, the flooding of the population with millions of leaflets dropped from the air, did not achieve our ends. For the present we must make a temporary retreat in order to re-organize and consolidate our forces. To this end an intensified programme of political training is necessary. To-day this is the most important task of the entire party.' Grotewohl then—it was still October 1946—produced the following Party directive: every year 180,000 members of the S.E.D. must receive political training in residential schools, to be achieved through the establishment of 130 Kreis Party schools for two-week courses with sixty Party members attending. This would ensure the political education of 187,600 members per year.

This gigantic plan was not quite fulfilled. Nevertheless, by the spring of 1948, 120 Kreis schools, six Land schools and one central Party school on a university level had been established; and almost 100,000 members of the Party had taken courses at these schools. Thus, without letting itself be influenced by its electoral reverses, the S.E.D. had succeeded in building up a solid core of functionaries by the spring of 1948.

The ideological education of the rank and file is effected by means of courses and organized (and supervised) private study; but the middle and higher appointments in all Stalinist Parties are occupied exclusively by functionaries who have completed prolonged courses in residential institutions. In Russia the Central Committee of the Party runs an Academy for Social Sciences, a Party High School, one-year special courses for secretaries of provincial Party committees, two-year Lenin courses, one-year courses for senior Party and State officials, six-month courses for secretaries of town and district Party committees. The Party central committees in all the Union republics have in addition their own Party educational institutions: some of the courses last as long as three years. It was announced in October 1952 that 35,000 Party functionaries were then studying in these schools, and that in the period 1947-52 400,000 functionaries had completed courses in residential institutions. In Eastern Germany there exist (apart from the 'Karl Marx' school and the Institute for Social Sciences), fifteen *Bezirksparteischulen* for one-year courses, and seventy *Kreisparteischulen* for three-month courses.

The Party High Schools for Advanced Study

The political training system in the Soviet zone (as in the Soviet Union) is set up on a hierarchical basis. From lower activities in evening classes, through the week-end and short-term courses at residential schools, Kreis and Bezirk schools, an ever increasing number of younger men are being politically ideologically trained, and the most active and capable are selected for advanced political study at the Party High Schools. I was, myself, associated with two of these high schools: the Komintern school in the Soviet Union from 1942 to 1943 (as student) and the Party High Schools of the S.E.D. from 1947 to 1949 in Klein-Machnow near Berlin (as instructor). The course at the S.E.D. Party High School takes three years; and five years are required at the Party High School of the Central Committee of the Communist Party of the Soviet Union, where only university graduates are accepted.

It would be a great mistake to judge the intellectual level of functionaries who have attended higher Party schools on the basis of the primitive propaganda pamphlets aimed at the masses.

The curriculum of these schools is by no means limited to the mouthing or memorizing of speeches by Party leaders or editorials in the press. It is on a very high level. It is definitely no mere formality that the schools are divided into various faculties (history, philosophy, political economy and problems of Marxism-Leninism) and put on a par with other universities.

In the Komintern school in 1942-3 the system of instruction was by courses of lectures. Lectures on certain important subjects such as the history of the Komintern and general questions of Marxism-Leninism, were given to the school as a whole. Otherwise each national section had its own curriculum. There were at the time twelve of these sections—Spanish, French, Italian, German, Austrian, Sudetan, Polish, Czech, Slovak, Hungarian, Roumanian and Bulgarian. There was also a section for Koreans but these were kept apart. Our special subjects in the German section were: Political economy, history of the U.S.S.R., of the K.P.D., of Fascism, the nature and course of World War II and the anti-fascist struggle in Hitler's Germany.

In the S.E.D.'s Higher Party School 'Karl Marx' instruction, in 1947-9, came under four main headings: Philosophy (primarily dialectical and historical materialism), History (in particular the German workers' movement and German Communist Party), Economics (especially the revelant works of Marx, Lenin and Stalin) and finally 'Basic Problems of Marxism-Leninism' (such as Class and Class struggle, the doctrine of the State, the doctrine of the Party, the role of the working class, strategy and tactics, the peasant question, Nationalism, and Colonialism. The curriculum has since been extended to include the history of the Russian Communist Party, economic and political geography, international relations, journalism, theory and history of art and literature, party organization and the Russian language.

The Party schools for advanced learning place great value on the careful study of 'enemy' ideologies. Thus at the Komintern school in 1942-3 we were made thoroughly acquainted with Nazi ideology. The history of the N.S.D.A.P., the Hitler Youth, and other Nazi organizations, as well as the biographies of the Nazi leaders, were presented to us in a long series of lectures. We studied Nazi ideology down to the last detail—the race theory, the 'Lebensraum' theory, the Nazi-concept of history, etc.—making use of Nazi literature itself. We made such a thorough study of these things that after 1945, when I met real Nazis, I discovered to my astonishment that I knew much more about their theory than they themselves did.

I was repeatedly surprised by the relative breadth of view and objectivity with which we dealt with Nazism and Nazi ideology in the Komintern school—in the middle of a war of life and death. Frequently one of the students was given an assignment to present certain theses of Nazi ideology to the group, while another had to produce arguments to invalidate the Nazi position. The student whose job it was to advance the Nazi arguments was instructed to make a clear and convincing presentation—the better he made out his case the higher his performance was assessed.

At the Party school 'Karl Marx', from 1947 to 1949, I personally observed the great value put on the study and refutation of 'enemy' theories and ideas. This time, however, the main emphasis was on bourgeois and social democratic ideology.

This study of opposition and enemy points of view was undertaken with particular zeal in the philosophy classes. The students were taught, with great thoroughness, how to refute the common interpretation of 'Marxist Determinism'; the relationship between logic and dialectic was given exhaustive treatment, and mimeographed material under the title 'Current attacks on Marxist Philosophy' which contained excerpts from bourgeois and social-democratic writings was regularly distributed.

At the higher Party schools therefore, the problems and theories formulated by the West—particularly in the sphere of philosophy and modern physics—were by no means suppressed but on the contrary received careful attention. The common assumption that all people in the Eastern countries are cut off from Western thought is no longer true in the case of higher functionaries. For example, at both the Komintern school and the Karl Marx school I regularly received Western newspapers, monitorings of Western broadcasts, speeches of Western government officials and leaders, programmes of Western political parties and the Papal encyclicals.

There is thus an important difference in the attitude of Communist government and Party leaders towards the education of the masses and of the functionaries. Vigorous steps are taken to keep Western influence away from the masses. In the case of functionaries being prepared for responsible Party positions, the policy is quite the opposite: one studies Western philosophies and theories with great thoroughness so that the future Party leaders may be immune from Western ways of thinking. It must be said that this policy in the vast majority of cases has proved itself successful.

The relative tolerance in respect to theories 'hostile to the Party' in the Party schools has one very marked limitation: publications and material on the Trotskyist and other Marxist opposition groups (and, after 1948, all Yugoslav material) are strictly forbidden. This is done, in my opinion, because it is from this quarter that the real danger threatens. In these writings a language is spoken which is familiar to the Party functionary but they contain critical thoughts which many functionaries secretly entertain. Arguments are brought forward in them which might convince or at least leave a deep impression.

The education of responsible functionaries does not only consist of academic study but also involves strict regulations in regard to conduct. For one thing, upon matriculation at the Komintern school, the student was given a new name, and was strictly instructed not to disclose his real name to anyone during the entire period at the school. The same system was used at the Party school 'Karl Marx' for all functionaries sent from West Germany to study there. There were two reasons for this measure in my opinion: firstly to prevent conspiracy. In the event of one of the graduates breaking with the Party, he would not be in a position to give personal data about his fellow students. Secondly, the giving of fictitious names made it clear to those participants who had held important posts in the government, Party or army that they were now transformed once more into simple students, and had only the Party to thank for their careers. Moreover, all use of alcohol in the Komintern school was strictly forbidden for the entire length of the course. Even at the New Year's Eve celebrations and on occasions such as November 7 or May 1 not a drop of alcohol was served. The same strict rules applied to contact with the other sex. Even the most innocent approaches—a short walk in the courtyard or in the school—were reported, and if repeated, were treated at length in the Criticism and Self-criticism sessions. An offence against these regulations led to expulsion from the school, and in some cases to immediate expulsion from the Party, with all the resulting consequences. The attempt is made, however, to avoid allowing these rigid rules to appear as repression but rather to give them an ideological basis and justification.

Just how strong a role is played by psychological influences in the education of the functionaries is shown by the process of 'Criticism and Self-criticism', which unfortunately has become an object of ridicule in the West. In reality it is the most effective method of ensuring absolute submission. The functionaries are disciplined not to keep anything from 'the Party', however private or personal. On certain evenings set aside for this purpose, an atmosphere is created which compels those present voluntarily to confess everything about themselves.

During my period at the Komintern school nearly all the members of our German section were subjected to such Criticism and Self-criticism sessions, which often lasted for five, six or more hours. Chance remarks, with the minimum of political implication, were appraised and analysed in unending interrogation till finally they were built up into 'political conceptions' or 'undesirable traits of character', of which the lamentable results were then brought to the notice of the victim and all others present in innumerable examples.

The importance of Criticism and Self-criticism at Party High School level is not to be underestimated. The great majority of the participants admit, as a matter of course, the right of the Party—in this case the accusers, acting in the name of the Party —to sit in judgment upon them, as upon any Party functionary. In so far as they are loyal to the Party line (which the great majority undoubtedly are), it would never occur to them to doubt the validity of the accusations, and they are filled with a profound sense of shame.

The efficacy of Self-criticism depends largely, if not wholly, on the degree in which the victim is permeated with Stalinist ideology. From my own experience I remember the quite shattering impression of my first Self-criticism in November 1942 in the Komintern school, when the charges against me were quite unfounded; and the negligible effect of my second in March 1949 in the Karl Marx school (just before my flight to Yugoslavia), although in the latter case oppositional utterances could in fact have been proved against me. The difference in the efficacy was not due to any difference in procedure—both sessions were conducted on very similar lines—but to the fact that I was no longer in the thrall of the main Stalinist ideological theses, and furthermore I knew the ideologically appropriate answers to the questions concerned.

Strict principles of behaviour and the psychological influence of Criticism and Self-criticism are not the only factors to explain the devotion to the Party of functionaries passing through the higher Party schools. There is also the feeling of gratitude at the trust in them displayed in the permission to read anti-Party literature. This is more important than may at first appear. For many functionaries it is a mark of distinction to belong to that circle to whom the Party can entrust the reading of such material. This privileged position in the graded scale of posses- sion of knowledge, the feeling of knowing so much more than the rank and file, is, to many functionaries, no less desirable than the titles, decorations and material privileges that come their way after passing through the schools. But the profound sense of devotion to and identification with the Party springs first and foremost from gratitude at having been found worthy of being prepared, in a Party school, for high Party tasks, grati- tude for the confidence thus shown, and a deep sense of obli- gation to prove that confidence justified; and pride at the thought of embarking on a life so superior to that of the common ruck, pre-occupied with personal and family affairs—the life of an activist, a conscious participant in historical process, one who in the Party and with the Party is changing the whole course of the future development of mankind.

Those who complete their courses at the higher Party schools are mostly appointed at once to responsible senior State and Party posts. As all my colleagues in the Komintern school bore assumed names I can only give a few examples, which however, I imagine are typical: Mischa Wolf became Counsellor of Embassy in the Eastern zone's mission in Moscow; Rudolf Dölling was made chief of the Political Directorate of the Volks-polizei; and Heinz Hoffmann was appointed Lieutenant General commanding the Police Militia (Kasernierte Volks-polizei) and deputy Minister of the Interior of the Eastern zone.

Among other evidence of the importance attached to the schools by the Party leadership is the fact that even the highest Party functionaries are seconded for service in them. In the Komintern school the German section was under the charge of Paul Wandel (there called Klassner) who had been Pieck's closest collaborator in the Komintern. In charge of the Polish section was Jacob Berman, now member of the Politburo of the Polish Party and deputy Prime Minister of Poland.

In the S.E.D. 'Karl Marx' higher Party school the courses started and finished with elaborate ceremonies, always attended by President Pieck, by Prime Minister Grotewohl or the first Secretary of the Central Committee, Walter Ulbricht. They did not, however, come only to the opening and end-of-course ceremonies: they gave addresses during the courses, in parti-cular at the time of any modification of the current Party line. Other Politburo members came (and still come) frequently, to give special lectures on developments and changes. They often emphasize that their remarks are for Party consumption only: and indeed much more is said on these occasions than is con-tained in the official Party hand-outs.

This extensive hierarchically-organized political school sys-tem has the following tasks:

1. By means of thorough and detailed study—including the counter-arguments for all possible 'Western' objections—the functionaries are made capable of justifying and presenting in a favourable light every line of policy adopted by the Soviet leadership.

2. By a regime of complete abstinence the functionary is 'pro-tected' from any deviations and brought to the point where he is completely and exclusively devoted to the service of the Party.

3. By the avoidance of any secret from the Party and the practice of Criticism and Self-Criticism (involving a constant feeling of guilt) the psychological dependence of each individual functionary on the Party is assured.

Through the interplay of these various factors—the acquisition of knowledge, a fundamental ascetic moral code and the process of Criticism and Self-criticism, the Party leadership has succeeded in building up a considerable number of well-trained cadres, completely dedicated to the Party. Of course there are other incentives. There are the material advantages (high salaries, exclusive use of certain restaurants, shops and health resorts) as well as the exceptional opportunities for promotion. Not a few high and even top positions are filled by men aged between 25 and 30. Nevertheless, it is my opinion that the decisive factor in the morale of functionaries is the combination of political instruction and psychological discipline in the Party schools. It should be pointed out that only a relatively small part of the population receives such training, but each year the number of loyal and devoted Party functionaries increases. Moreover, this particular group is the most active part of the population and has its hands on all key positions in every social field. With each graduating class, an ever larger portion of the population comes under this influence. The character of their training explains the attitude of many functionaries—an attitude which is otherwise quite incomprehensible to people in the West. I have known a considerable number of functionaries whose parents or nearest relatives were arrested or even shot in the Soviet Union, but who continued to be loyal servants of the system. I further know of a few functionaries who were themselves imprisoned in the Soviet Union, but after their release returned to East Berlin where they are still active supporters of the regime.

Political Stomach-Aches

On the other hand I by no means want to give the impression that the training invariably works as an effective miracle drug. It should not be overlooked that the Party schools do not only raise dedicated and true disciples of Stalinism; at the same time, contrary to the intention of their initiators, they produce the most effective opponents and dangerous heretics.

When and how is it possible for a schooled ideological functionary to break with Stalinism? How does such a break take place? What are the decisive problems involved? What are the motives? A break with Stalinism is not a single act, but rather

77

the result of a long process over a period of years, a continuous spiral of doubts and justifications, until the decisive point has been reached at which the break is made.

Let us restrict our discussion of political doubts and reservations to ideological functionaries, although they play a considerable role in the case of other types of official. Such doubts and reservations are seldom based on personal experience or the questioning of the correctness of certain specific policies (for example, the Oder-Niesse border, dismantling etc.) or current political measures (e.g. negotiations with Adenauer). They are rather of a fundamentally ideological character. Not until the functionary in question becomes aware of the fact that certain events or measures contradict the fundamental teachings of Marx, Engels and Lenin, does he start to doubt; these initial doubts lead him to conscious opposition. A possible historical comparison might lie with certain of the disputes among mediaeval Scholastic philosophers, or the ideological conflicts of the initial phase of the Reformation period. Of course the comparison should not be pushed too far.

Among Eastern functionaries, a special term is in current use for doubts, reservations, and conceptions not in tune with the official Party line: 'Political Stomach-Aches'. Most functionaries keep their stomach troubles to themselves. Some of them discuss their troubles in sworn secrecy with their closest friends. Despite their diversity, these individual deviations have a common characteristic: they have virtually nothing to do with 'Western' arguments or a Western 'way of life'. They are rather an expression of the conflict of interpretation within the system itself, of a differentiation between the teachings of Marx and Lenin on the one hand and of Stalinist and post-Stalinist theory and practice on the other.

Below are listed some of the most important questions which again and again are discussed among functionaries in talks 'strictly between ourselves':

1. The dependence of the S.E.D. (or the comparable party of another country) on the Soviet Union and the C.P.S.U., in contradiction to the independence of the socialist workers' movement in each country demanded by Marx and Engels.

2. The Stalinist thesis that all People's Democracies should follow the example set by the Soviet Union in contradiction to the fundamental principle proclaimed by Marx and Engels according to which development towards socialism is to be based on the particular economic, political and cultural conditions in each country.

3. The Stalinist principle of continuously strengthening the authority of the State in the U.S.S.R. and the Soviet Bloc countries, in contradiction to the teaching of Marx and Engels that the socialist development will lead towards a weakening and final death of the State.

4. The omnipotence of the directors of state-owned enterprises in the Soviet Union and the Soviet bloc countries, in contradiction to the management of industrial enterprises by elected workers' committees demanded by Marx and Engels for the socialist society.

5. The suppression of freedom of opinion in the Party, which the younger generation becomes sharply aware of when they read in Lenin's writings of the frank and free discussions which were common practice in the Bolshevik Party of earlier days.

6. The enormous privileges of the functionaries in Party, government and industry, contrary to the teachings of Marx, Engels and Lenin, whereby no one may receive 'compensation exceeding that of a worker's wage' in a socialist society.

7. The steadily increasing force of suppression, contradicting the principle formulated by Marx, Engels and Lenin, that the limitations of freedom should only be considered a temporary measure against the exploiter classes and must be lifted, after these classes have been overthrown, and replaced by the guarantee of extensive freedom for all working people.

The above-mentioned 'political stomach-aches' show that it is among those elements which grew up under Stalinism and became saturated with Stalinist ideology that opposition springs up, from a Marxist standpoint, as a defence of true and pure Marxism against Stalinism which twisted and reversed the teachings of Marx and Engels.

The Effect of 'Western' Propaganda

Since I have been in the West, I have often been asked what effect the Western propaganda has had on people like my friends and myself—that is, the younger generation of independently thinking and oppositionally minded ideological functionaries. My questioners are usually astounded when I say that we read Western newspapers every day and frequently listened to broadcasts; but that this Western propaganda had practically no effect on us as 'ideological functionaries'. On the contrary it tended to delay our breaking with Stalinism, rather than speeding up such a break.

We could condemn 'the unscientific formulation used in the Western press' in our circles. Since all political terms such as people, democracy, freedom, nation, Socialism, etc., had a definite meaning for us, every use of these terms which did not correspond to our definition seemed to us to be 'unscientific' and written by people who 'did not know the first thing about political science', as we used to express it. The really significant events which stimulated intense discussion among us and about which we would have been eager to read a serious Western commentary, were usually not even mentioned. 'They do not seem to have any idea of what is going on', was the tenor of our conversations about the Western press. Instead, the West Berlin and West German newspapers regularly brought detailed and gloating reports on local shortages in the Soviet zone. Thus we always experienced a double disappointment: the important issues which we would stay up all night discussing and which were the cause of our 'political stomach-aches' were rarely touched upon; while relatively unimportant shortages and insufficiencies were played up. It was just this kind of thing which seemed unjust to us and in such instances we again felt a kinship with the system in the face of these attacks. Our reaction was understandable.

Descriptions of better living conditions in the west or facts about higher hourly wages for the worker were, according to my experience, completely without effect on persons trained in Stalinist schools. We had already been provided with the counter argument: such a comparison is invalid at the present date because the transformation of society always involves temporary sacrifices and material difficulties.

Equally ineffectual were descriptions of the tragic personal fate of persons in the East. As a part of the ABC of Stalinist political education one learns that in evaluating social conditions one must look not to the fate of individuals, but rather to historical development.

Particularly fatal is the effect of the tone of contempt, mockery and irony used by the Western press in discussing matters which are sacred even to the opposition-minded functionary—for example reference to the Great Socialist October Revolution as a 'Putsch' or personal attacks on Lenin.

Also the broadcast attempts at the 'Refutation of Marxism', so often accompanied by a sarcastic undertone, is apt to make the functionaries smile, as they usually know much more about Marxism than does the commentator. The same applies to the propaganda effect of 'Western' terminology such as 'Western Christendom' or 'private enterprise', etc.

It should never be forgotten that, among the younger generation in particular, even sharp opposition to the Stalinist system very seldom involves an acceptance of the Western system. All attempts to shake Party ideology by means of propaganda for the Western system are futile when directed to schooled functionaries. Very many opponents of Stalinism would reject propaganda which urges restitution of large landed estates, the return of firms to their former owners, the re-introduction of the former parties, or the systematic application of the Western system to Eastern countries.

The main tenor of Western propaganda by radio or leaflets can, in my opinion, only influence such people as are not yet greatly influenced by Stalinism. It has no effect on the strata which actually counts in ideological conflict, on the younger people raised up under Stalinism and who are permeated with the Party ideology.

The Ideological Functionary after Stalin's Death

In closing a few words must be said about the significance of ideology and the ideological functionary in the present period —that is since the death of Stalin.

In the West one is naturally inclined to pay greatest attention to Soviet external policy. However, the internal changes have an even greater significance for the future development of the Soviet Union and the Eastern Bloc nations: important features being the curtailment of the power of the State Security Service, open criticism of it in the press and in the theatre, and its subordination to the Party and government leadership; the end of the cult of the leader and the establishment of the principle of collective leadership; the strong emphasis on equal rights for the various peoples of the Soviet Union; the apparent change in attitude toward the satellites, the visit of the Soviet leaders to Belgrade and the resulting recognition (at least in words) of the right of countries to move towards socialism in their own way; the decentralization of the economy, including the transfer of more than 24,000 centrally administered firms to the Union Republics; the giving of awards to old Bolshevists, who under Stalin were forced out of public life, and even arrested; a definite, if still limited, relaxation of restrictions in the fields of literature and music, and the renunciation of Stalin's ostentatious architecture; and finally the frank admission that the Soviet Union can learn from other countries.

These developments are doubtless partly due to the 'contradictions' which the Soviet Union found itself faced with after the death of Stalin: the Stalinist foreign policy had led to

national isolation; Stalin's Russification policy had produced
tensions between Russians and the non-Russian national states;
the absolute domination of the State Security Service had produced serious discontent within leading Party and government
circles; the over-centralization of the economy had smothered
local initiative; the 'leader cult' had become a superstitious
deification of authority, and the complete insulation against
Western influences had resulted in a standstill of scientific and
intellectual development. On the other hand, industrialization
and the sociological changes necessarily involved (for example
the emergence of a skilled technical intelligentsia, an army
officer corps, etc. etc.) had created both the objective pre-
requisites and the subjective forces which made necessary a
change in the Stalinist course—a change which in any case
would have come about earlier or later, but was doubtless
hastened by Stalin's death.

The extent and significance of the changes can not yet be
finally determined. However, the measures introduced since
Stalin's death seem more than mere tactical tricks. But they do
not yet justify talk of a transformation of the entire system,
which now as ever retains the rule of bureaucracy over the
nationalized means of production and over all political and
cultural fields. The changes could perhaps best be described as
a process of de-Stalinization; since they indicate important
modifications in domestic and economic policy, nationality and
foreign policy, but do not touch on the fundamentals of the
system. It may be the goal of the post-Stalin Soviet leadership
not to change the system itself, but to free it of 'superfluous'
Stalinist points of friction, in order to make it function more
smoothly and effectively. At present it is not possible to foresee
whether the changes will remain within the framework of the
set goal. It might be that the current process of de-Stalinization
will at some future date lead to a transformation in the system
itself—of course, for the present, only vague conjectures are
possible on this topic. So far it has been solely a matter of
changes within the system created by Stalin.

In commentaries in the Western press about developments
in the Soviet Union since the death of Stalin, I have frequently
encountered the concept that these changes are for the most
part inspired and executed by the 'realists', while the 'ideologists' on the other hand, are a retarding and hindering force.
This distinction between the 'good realists' (presumably the
leading forces in the economic bureaucracy and perhaps army)
and the 'bad ideologists' is one I have never been able to share.

In my many years of experience as a Party functionary I have found that the dividing line between the strictly dogmatic, 100-per-cent Stalinists on the one side, and the open-minded, independent and progressive functionaries on the other is not connected with their specific functions; this division cuts through all spheres (government, Party, army, etc.). I personally have found more independent thinkers and open-minded function-aries among the 'ideologists' (that is, the trained party function-aries) than among those in the government and in industry. This may be coincidence, and my own experiences certainly do not justify final conclusions. Yet the frequent division into 'bad ideologists' and 'good realists' should in my opinion be used with extreme caution.

There is a further point. My own interpretation is that the present process of de-Stalinization in the U.S.S.R. does not mean (nor is ever likely to mean) that the whole leading class is turning away from ideology and approaching a 'policy of realism'; but rather that the ideology itself is undergoing a change. In other words I would maintain that the practical steps taken have their foundation in changes in the ideology. It is a well-known fact that a distinction is always made in the U.S.S.R. between so-called fundamentals and current prob-lems, and ultimately the former is always decisive. It seems to me that a state like the U.S.S.R., whose domestic and foreign policy, whose economic policy, whose entire existence is governed by ideological motivating principles can only break with Stalinism in practice if this is concurrent with a renuncia-tion of the ideology of Stalinism.

Such has been the case so far. The switch from the personal cult over to the idea of collective achievement, for example, has not only been implemented in practice but has been given ideological foundation (by the re-writing of certain history books and by ideological articles on the significance of the masses in history).

Recent philosophical congresses seem to me to be particularly significant in this connection, such as were held early in 1955 in the Institute of Philosophy of the Academy of Sciences in the U.S.S.R., at the Party Institute and at the Lenin Military Academy. At these sessions a number of questions were raised which formerly had been considered as finally 'solved', which had been 'answered' by Stalin, and which, until then, no Soviet philosopher had dared approach. With astonishing frankness such problems as contradictions in the Soviet society were dis-cussed, the 'completely impossible planning of scientific work' criticized, the necessity for an earnest study of Western philosophy was pointed out; and it was frankly admitted that many philosophers had, until now, avoided—as one avoids fire—the search for a new solution to this or that problem. 'They were afraid to question the established dogma.'

It is interesting to note that this time—in contrast to the 'discussions' under Stalin's leadership—reports of the proceedings did not appear in the daily press, but were published in a specialized journal. Apparently it is thought best to limit the presentation of new problems to an ideological élite. Yet even with this limitation the importance of these discussions should not be underestimated. It is still impossible to give a final answer to the question of how far and how deep this reversal of the ideology of Stalinism will be. But the mere fact that such a process has begun must be considered of great significance— not only for the people of the Soviet Union, but also for the people of the whole world.

THE RUSSIANS AND THE EAST GERMAN PARTY

(PRELUDE TO JUNE 17TH 1953)

By George Sherman

I

THE events in the Soviet-occupied zone of Germany on June 16-17 cannot be taken in isolation from the whole course of Communist policy in that area after 1945. To a large extent the 'June days' reflected the bitterness and despair engendered by that policy, while their timing and, indeed, the fact that they could even occur, were due to its latest turn—namely, the introduction of the 'New Course' in the zone on June 11, 1953. Therefore, before going into the main body of the paper it is desirable to give a survey of the developments during the years between 1945 and 1953.

The Soviet Union came to Germany as one of three victorious occupying powers who pledged themselves to follow a concerted policy of 'democratization, demilitarization and denazification'. Central power in Germany, as worked out at Potsdam, was vested in the Allied Control Council of the four military governors sitting in Berlin. However, the provision that all council decisions must be unanimous to be binding safeguarded the prerogatives of each state in its own zone. It soon became apparent that the Soviet interpretation of the Potsdam formula served aims which were at variance with those conceived by the Western Allies; and the continued unilateral implementation of Soviet policy assured the breakdown of Allied co-operation and hence the division of Germany.

Beginning with Yalta, the Soviet government had consistently demanded German reparations to the sum of ten billion dollars. Though the Western Powers had never agreed to this sum, they had agreed at Yalta on the right to reparations, and on the methods by which they were to be extracted. After no further agreement could be reached, it was decided at Potsdam that each power should satisfy its reparations demands principally from its own zone—presumably by those methods outlined at Yalta, though they were not explicitly mentioned again at

Potsdam. At the same time it was agreed that Germany should be treated as an economic whole; to this end a number of central German administrations were to be established under the aegis of the Allied Control Council. On the basis of these rather loose agreements, and through directives issued by the Allied Control Council regarding the permitted peace-time level of German basic industry, the dismantling of German plants was begun in all zones in 1945. However, it soon developed that there could be no question of long-termed agreement on reparations, because of the varying emphasis the different powers placed on the relationship between reparations and German economic stability.

For the Western powers, and especially the United States, the implementation of the agreement to treat Germany as an economic unit became a prerequisite for the extraction of reparations. While it was agreed that unneeded war potential and excess production could be taken as reparations, the West insisted more and more adamantly that this go hand-in-hand with a well-functioning economy able to maintain a viable standard of living for the Germans. In addition to sharing the general Western desire to avoid a disastrous reparations policy similar to that following World War I, the Americans more particularly feared that they would bear a large share of the reparations burden in an economically divided and unstable Germany. If zonal divisions remained and the excessive Russian demands on Germany were to be met, money and goods would simply flow into the American zone and out again eastwards to pay the Russian reparations. If this were to be avoided, first a German economy must be established capable of paying its own reparations.

The Russian approach, on the other hand, tended in quite the opposite direction. First and foremost, they wanted reparations; from the first days of their occupation they set about extracting them on the widest scale possible. Whole plants and their machinery were dismantled, personal property and livestock were confiscated—all for immediate shipment to the Soviet Union. On July 9, 1946, Molotov underscored this importance of reparations to the Soviet government when he announced in a speech at the Paris meeting of the Council of Foreign Ministers that the insurance of reparations deliveries was one of the main reasons for occupying Germany. The overriding singlemindedness with which the Russians carried out the exploitation of their zone, coupled with their continued demands for a share in carrying out a similar process in the

Western zones, demonstrates that—unlike the Western Allies—they had little intention of resurrecting a healthy self-sustaining economy. Quite the contrary—their dual aim was to destroy once and for all the German threat to Russia through a decisive crippling of the economy, and to channel the confiscated German resources into the rehabilitation of the war-devastated Soviet economy. Though the conditions of four-power occupation made impossible the direct implementation of this policy everywhere in the country, the Russians initially sought to achieve its purpose outside their zone by committing the Western Allies to guarantee exorbitant reparations under the guise of 'economic and military disarmament of Germany'. This proved impossible as continued unilateral Soviet measures in their zone and their almost exclusive pre-occupation with reparations revealed the cross-purposes at which the various occupying powers were working.

During the prolonged occupation which ensued from the breakdown of co-operation, the Soviet Union pursued twin aims: to hinder in every way possible the economic and political unity of the Western zones, while establishing a strong Communist position in its own zone. There was a continued concentration on reparations at least until 1948, but their extraction became far more organized. The initial unco-ordinated dismantling and confiscation proved economically inefficient, hindered the establishment of any kind of rudimentary order, and raised obstacles to the long-run consolidation of the Communist position by completely alienating the zonal population. Hence after 1946 there was a growing emphasis on the establishment of Soviet-owned corporations (S.A.G.s) in Eastern Germany; instead of dismantling, plants were maintained in Germany under complete Soviet control and their goods produced for direct shipment to the Soviet Union.[1] At the same time, the Soviet Military Administration effected economic and social measures which in their later implementation assured a monopoly of political power to the German Communist proteges. If the Western zones could be kept politically disunited and economically dislocated under the guise of the Potsdam Agreement, then the Communist-controlled zone might form the base for future domination of the whole country. At the least, such a policy guaranteed the much-needed reparations and a certain influence in the future development of even an

---

[1] Cf. Vladimir Rudolph, 'The Administrative Organization of Soviet Control, 1945-1948: B. The Execution of Policy, 1945-1947', *Soviet Economic Policy in Postwar Germany* (New York 1953), pp. 36-61.

independent Germany—through the paramount Communist position in only a part of the country and the irrevocable measures taken unilaterally there.

Although the end product of developments in both Eastern Europe and the Soviet zone of Germany was their complete subordination to the interests of the Soviet Union, the forms of control and the timing of their implementation in Germany were determined by a set of somewhat different factors. Not only were various facets of Soviet policy in the zone contradictory to one another, but also they contradicted wider aims toward the whole of occupied Germany. For instance, the desire to establish effective Communist control in the zone was continually frustrated by popular reaction against the wholesale pilfering carried out through reparations; at the same time, the necessity to maintain some appeal to all-German national feelings and to hinder Allied unity in Western Germany caused the sovietization of zonal society to take devious routes which were quite unnecessary in establishing Communist domination of the Eastern European states.

In Germany, measures which were to form the basis for future Communist control of the zone were initially pursued in the name of the Potsdam formula for reconstruction. In May and June 1945 the Soviet Union had already taken the lead among the occupying powers in setting up local administrations under the supervision of the Soviet commandants. They were largely organized through the efforts of two groups of German Communists, ten men each, who had been flown from their wartime exile in Moscow to carry out this specific task. While these functionaries took great care in placing Communists at the heart of these administrations, they repeatedly publicized their aim of engaging all non-Nazi talent in a co-operative effort to resurrect efficient administrative bodies.[2] As agreed at Potsdam, these bodies were given increasing responsibility in administering the routine affairs of the zone.

On June 10, 1945, the Soviet Military Administration in its Order No. 2 under the authority of Marshall Zhukov permitted the establishment of anti-fascist political parties and trade union organizations. These groups, which were to aid in rooting-out the vestiges of Nazism, must register with the S.M.A. and operate under its control.[3] The top German Communists were

[2] Cf. Wolfgang Leonhard, *Die Revolution entlässt Ihre Kinder* (Cologne and Berlin 1955), pp. 334-89. The author, who flew to Berlin as part of the 'Ulbricht group', gives a detailed account of that group's activities in the first weeks of May 1945.
[3] The Order is reprinted in full in Walter Ulbricht: *Zur Geschichte der neuesten Zeit* (Berlin 1955), pp. 368-9.

advised of this step beforehand; consequently they were able to reconstitute the German Communist Party three days later on the basis of a programme recently brought back from Moscow by the high German functionary, Wilhelm Pieck.[4] The temperate tone and limited aims of this declaration, together with the rapidity with which the Russians had acted in resurrecting broad political activity in their zone, were well calculated to reassure the Western Allies, as well as German opinion, about Communist aims in Germany.

According to the new Communist programme, the destruction of Nazi Germany had created the opportunity for continuing the 'bourgeois-democratic' (bürgerlich-demokratische) transformation begun by the revolution of 1848. Feudal vestiges, such as huge landholdings and reactionary Prussian militarism, must be decisively removed to aid in the establishment of democracy. In the ten immediate tasks outlined for the German people, the party went so far as to call for the resurrection of an economic system based on private enterprise. Land was to be redistributed to private peasants ruined and without property from the war; there was no mention of collectivization of agriculture. The only explicitly socialist aim announced was an elemental one common to all socialist parties: The taking over by the reconstituted provincial and district administrations of all those undertakings which serve the most important needs of life—transport, water, gas and electric works. Any other socialization would occur only if the owners had deserted their property, except of course for Nazis and war criminals—their possessions were to be confiscated *en toto*.[5]

The most important passage of the programme rejected quite emphatically any intention of using the Soviet model for Germany:

We are of the opinion that it would be the wrong way to force the Soviet system on Germany, for this way does not correspond to the present conditions of development in Germany.

We are much more of the opinion that the decisive interests of the German people in the present situation prescribe another way for Germany, the way of the erection of an anti-fascist democratic regime, of a parliamentary-democratic republic with all the democratic rights and freedoms for the people.[6]

[4] Wolfgang Leonhard, *op. cit.*, pp. 389-401.
[5] The programme is reprinted in Walter Ulbricht, *op. cit.*, pp. 370-9.
[6] Walter Ulbricht, *op. cit.*, p. 375.

This section coincided with the strict admonitions given the German Communist emigrés in Moscow as early as January 1945. They were told that they must remember at all times that Allied and Russian unity had won the war, that this unity would be maintained in administering the defeated Germany, and that there could be no talk of socialism in carrying out agreed directives. There must be a constant struggle against 'sectarianism'; the Communists as a group would have real meaning only in so far as they were individual members of a block of anti-fascist elements created to help the wartime Allies re-establish democracy in Germany.[7]

The ideological foundation for this tactic of the German Communists was embodied in the so-called 'Ackermann Thesis' —named after its author, Party ideologist Anton Ackermann. In a theoretical article, which appeared in the December 1945 issue of the official Party journal *Einheit*, Ackermann based himself on Marx and Lenin in answering affirmatively the question —'Is there a special German way to socialism?' Marx had foreseen the possibility of a peaceful transition to socialism in those countries which possessed 'bourgeois-democratic' forms of government without an especially pronounced militarism or bureaucracy. Although Marx had limited this analysis to England and the United States, Ackermann concluded it would be wrong to exclude all lands under all circumstances. Germany must be in this category now, since the war had destroyed the old militarism and bureaucracy. If the new 'anti-fascist-democratic' republic could develop under the leadership of the working class, then socialism could be achieved peacefully. In postulating that forms and methods of this leadership must be German and not Soviet, Ackermann based himself on Lenin's caution against exaggerating the particular characteristics of the Russian revolution into general truths about all revolution. He followed this up by contrasting the social development of Russia in 1917 with that of Germany in 1945. Russia had been a backward country with a low level of industrial production from a proletariat which was a minority of the population. On the other hand, Germany in 1945 possessed a highly-developed industry run by a qualified working force that comprised a majority of the whole population. Hence, Ackermann concluded that the construction of socialism in Germany would involve far less material sacrifice, far less inner political strife; there could be 'a special German Way to Socialism'.[8] It appeared from this thesis, as well as from the Party programme,

[7] Wolfgang Leonhard, *op. cit.*, pp. 325-7.   [8] *Id.*, pp. 419-22.

that the German Communists' allegiance and loyalty to Moscow were going to be allowed to take independent forms.

The 'Ackermann Thesis' was propounded at the beginning of the Communist campaign for amalgamation with the Social Democratic Party (S.P.D.). In reality, one of its chief uses was to assuage the fears of those on the left—Social Democrats and local Communists—who opposed too great a dependence of a single Socialist Party on Moscow. The initial advantages enjoyed by the Communists in political organization and material help extended by the S.M.A. in the form of extra rations, housing, and transport had led them to reject in June 1945 the creation of a unified party with the Social Democrats. However, by the end of 1945 it was evident that the benefits of the political freedom allowed in the zone were being reaped by the S.P.D. and the two liberal democratic parties, and not by the K.P.D. as had been planned. The initial advantage of a close liaison with the occupying power had quickly turned into a great disadvantage, as the population transferred its dissatisfaction with Soviet plundering to the local Communists. The resulting growth in S.P.D. organizations throughout the zone, together with the decisive defeat administered the Communist Party in Austria in November 1945, lead to a reassessment of the former Communist position on fusion. This resulted in a decision to swallow the opposition on the left before the first provincial elections in the zone scheduled for October 1946.

The subsequent founding of the Socialist Unity Party (S.E.D.), which took place on April 21-22, 1946, at a joint congress of over one thousand S.P.D. and K.P.D. delegates, was the direct result of a high-powered Communist campaign which successfully combined force and persuasion. Unremitting pressure was applied to the higher echelons of the S.P.D. in the zone, and the membership was never permitted the opportunity to sanction the moves finally taken by the top. A proposed referendum among the S.P.D. membership in Berlin was outlawed in the Soviet sector; when it was held in the three Western sectors on March 31, a large majority opposed immediate amalgamation. During March and early April the Soviet commandants in the various provinces often took the lead in uniting the two party organizations into one—always from the top down. Finally, many S.P.D. delegates who were known to be opposed to unity were either arrested or refused admittance to the founding Congress on April 21.[9]

---

[9] Wolfgang Leonhard, *op. cit.*, pp. 423-42, gives a detailed account of the progress of this unity campaign from his own experiences.

Despite the admittedly important, if not decisive, role played by the use of such force, it cannot be denied that the call for a single socialist party had a genuine appeal. In fact, in June 1945 many leading Social Democrats had taken the lead in calling for such a party. There was general sentiment in both parties for eradicating the old divisions and antagonisms that had proved so costly up to 1933. Though the Communist leadership had initially rejected the overtures, every attempt had been made to establish a working co-operation between the two parties. The course of Soviet activities during 1945 and Communist affiliation with it may have cooled Social Democratic sentiment, but the constant reiteration of the 'Ackermann Thesis' with all its implications for an independent German Socialist Party had the reassuring effect desired. The Communists emphasized that the fusion was only one step further in the co-operation that already existed, and acquiesced readily to Social Democratic demands for freedom of discussion and election in the future party.[10]

The immediate organization of the new party seemed to bear out the Communist contention that little would be changed. The party apparatuses were simply merged. Each position was allotted on a parity basis; where one man had performed a function previously, it was now done by two—one Social Democrat and one Communist. The executive in charge of this swollen apparatus was a fourteen-man Central Secretariat —seven from the S.P.D. and seven from the K.P.D., while policy-making power was nominally invested in an eighty-man Party Committee—once again evenly divided between the two parties. Two chairmen were named by the founding congress: former head of the K.P.D., Wilhelm Pieck, and former head of the zonal S.P.D., Otto Grotewohl. Given this organization and the inclusion of the thesis of a 'special German Way to Socialism' within the Party statute, the S.P.D. leaders might well have been justified in believing they could exercise a more moderating influence in partnership than in opposition.

Where this enchantment existed, it could not have lasted long. The S.E.D. soon became the platform in Germany for the official Soviet line. Any freedom it may have been promised was strictly limited in practice within bounds set by the developing inflexibility of Soviet policy. This inflexibility emerged most clearly with the founding of the Cominform in Warsaw in September 1947; especially in the 'hard' line expounded then by Andrei Zhdanov, Party Secretary of the Communist Party

[10] *Id.*, p. 426.

of the Soviet Union; and in the expulsion of Tito from the Eastern European bloc in June 1948 for failing to submit unconditionally to Soviet authority. This rise of 'Zhdanovism' in late 1947 and early 1948, and its accelerated implementation after the break with Tito, meant the steady moulding of the S.E.D. into its Soviet prototype and the renunciation of the independent ideological base upon which it had been established. Accordingly, in the autumn of 1948 Ackermann was forced to recant and the doctrine of a 'German Way to Socialism' was shelved.

The reorganization of the leading organs was begun at the First Party Conference in January 1949, when it was decided to replace the Central Secretariat with a Politbureau. While the parity principle was retained, it was not applied to this new body. Four of the seven full members were former Communists; the two candidates were divided between the two former parties.[11] The parity principle was finally dropped altogether at the Third S.E.D. Congress in July 1950 with the acceptance of a set of statutes which brought organization virtually into conformity with that of the Communist Party of the Soviet Union (C.P.S.U.). The Politbureau was enlarged to nine full members, of which all save two were former Communists,[12] and the unwieldy Party Committee was replaced by a smaller Central Committee. Moscow Communist Walter Ulbricht was appointed to the new post of Secretary General, whereby official recognition was given to his supreme position in the 'Party of the New Type'—the creation of which he had openly backed since September 1947. The purge of the lower ranks during the early months of 1951—which followed from the decisions of the Third Party Congress—reduced membership to a number more consonant with that considered necessary for the proper functioning of such a ruling party. At the same time the purge served to renew the removal of 'oppositional' elements hostile to the Soviet Union which had been begun by the newly-established Party Control Commission in September 1948.

[11] The membership of the first Politbureau was as follows: Full members—Wilhelm Pieck (K.P.D.), Otto Grotewohl (S.P.D.), Walter Ulbricht (K.P.D.), Franz Dahlem (K.P.D.), Frederich Ebert (S.P.D.), Helmut Lehmann (S.P.D.), Paul Merker (K.P.D.); Candidate members—Anton Ackermann (K.P.D.); Karl Steinhof (S.P.D.).

[12] In the new Politbureau, Lehmann and Merker were dropped altogether, and four Communists were added to the full members remaining: Herman Matern, Fred Oelssner, Heinrich Rau, and Wilhelm Zaisser. The six candidates were all Communists: Anton Ackermann, Rudolph Herrnstadt, Elli Schmidt, Hans Jenchetzky, Erich Honecker, and Erich Mueckenberger.

This shaping of the S.E.D. into a pliant tool of Moscow paralleled its ascendancy to a monopoly of political power in the zone. Once again, this development contrasted sharply with the aims and promises held out in 1945. The Communist Party Manifesto in June had ended with an appeal for the creation of a 'block of anti-fascist democratic parties' which would co-operate in achieving the broad and not unacceptable aims set forth in the programme. The moderation of this pro-gramme and the restraint shown in actions—e.g. the creation by the Communists of broadly representative local administra-tive organs—together with obvious support given the 'block' policy by the occupying power, made the initially less active political groups unable to resist the appeal for co-operation. The Russians had predetermined what groups would form the block; by July, they had resurrected three more political parties in the zone—the Social Democratic Party (S.P.D.), the Chris-tian Democratic Union (C.D.U.), and the Liberal Democratic Party (L.D.P.). On July 14, 1945, their object was achieved when these three parties united with the K.P.D. to form the 'anti-fascist democratic Unity Front'. Through the emphasis on 'anti-fascism' and 'democracy' the Russians and German Com-munists could parade as champions of a genuine supra-party group formed to aid in attaining generally-agreed ends above the realm of political controversy.

The Soviet Military Administration now set about directing German implementation of previously-decided anti-fascist measures. At first they were on safe ground, for their reform measures were in such a direction as to raise a minimum of opposition either in the zone or among the Western Allies. In their inception, if not in the later course of their implementation, these first actions largely carried out by the Communist nucleus received at least passive support from the block members. The most significant such action was the comprehensive land reform of 1945, designed to break up the Junker estates and thereby remove one of the 'feudal vestiges' cited in the Communist programme. While German opinion may have varied about confiscation without compensation, there was general agree-ment about the value of redistributing the land among the private peasants. Also in the same category, the general confis-cation by the local administrations of the industrial and other holdings of all Nazis and war criminals was not carried out throughout the zone until a referendum held in Saxony in June 1946 had shown overwhelming support for it there.

With the breakdown of Allied and Soviet co-operation in

Germany and the concurrent emergence of Communist designs on the political life of the zone, the 'anti-fascist democratic Unity Front' revealed itself as a façade for associating all responsible political groups with unilateral Communist acts. No member of the block was permitted freedom of manoeuvre in opposing an official act perpetrated in the name of 'democratizing' or 'denazifying'. Such opposition was liable to be labelled 'fascist', following the simple dictum: He who is not for us must be against us. By identifying the Communist cause with the anti-fascist cause from the early days of the occupation, and by this later manipulating of loose terms to fit their more radical aims, the Russians were able to silence all opposition and effect their desired totalitarian development of the zone. S.P.D. opposition was dispelled through the operation of the S.E.D. and the 'liberal bourgeois' parties were moulded into useful mouthpieces, not only for the Communist policy in the zone, but also for recurrent Soviet appeals to all-German nationalism. This compliancy of the leadership of the liberal democratic parties was assured by December 1947, when Jacob Kaiser and his deputy, Ernst Lemmer—both of whom had remained public critics of Communist policy—were removed from their leadership of the C.D.U. through direct intervention by the Soviet Military Administration. Their passing signalized the end of any organized political opposition in the zone. On the other side, the propagation of the zonal two-year construction plan by Ulbricht at the Second S.E.D. Congress in September 1947; and then the acceptance of the five-year plan for the 'Deutsche Democratische Republik' (D.D.R.) by the Third Party Congress in 1950—together with Pieck's reference there to the S.E.D. as the government Party responsible for the fate of the republic—indicate the exclusive position of power delegated to the Communists.

In the light of this constant trend toward complete Communist domination of the zone, it is doubtful whether an influential part of the hierarchy—German and Soviet—ever considered the thesis of an 'independent German Way to Socialism' and the initial moves toward co-operation as more than tactical weapons fitted to the exigencies of the first days of four-powered occupation of Germany. Certainly, there is evidence that Walter Ulbricht never had any illusions on this score in 1945. After explaining the startlingly new programme to a group of eighty Communist functionaries in Berlin in that first week in June, he was unexpectedly asked to clarify how it differed from the platform of the usual 'bourgeois democratic' party. Ulbricht replied with a wink and a smile, the meaning of which no one present could misunderstand: 'That you will soon see, Comrade! Just you wait a little while!' (Das wirst du schon bald merken, Genosse! Wart nur mal ein bisschen ab!)[13] As the purely ideological aims of the Communists in the zone came into undisguised prominence during 1948 accompanied by the steady consolidation of Soviet type state control, the full import of such a remark uttered at such an early date by the future Secretary General of the S.E.D. cannot be under-estimated.

Despite the steady accretion of power to the S.E.D., its supremacy was imposed and guarded from the top by the Soviet Military Administration. The Party was nothing more than an administrative adjunct to the occupying power and every aspect of its policy was tightly bound to the overall German policy pursued by the Soviet Union. For this reason, Ulbricht and his sympathizers were not permitted until 1952 to carry their supremacy on the internal political scene to its natural extreme of sovietizing the zone.

It is true that the Russians had proceeded to exploit their zone economically and politically, and that this had tended toward the establishment of a Soviet-like system of controls. While thus violating Potsdam themselves, they had railed against every attempt of the Allies to unify separately the Western half of the country. They had gone to the extent of blockading Berlin in 1948 and part of 1949 with the dual aim of forcing the Western Allies out of a valuable vantage point in the Soviet zone, and of making them negotiate about the formation of the West German federal government. When this manoeuvre failed and the Bonn government came into being in May 1949, the Russians retaliated in the following October by almost spontaneously establishing the 'Deutsche Demo-kratische Republik' (D.D.R.). The act was so timed as to place the onus on the Western powers for dividing Germany between rival governments; however, the founding of the 'D.D.R.' was actually a natural consequence of approval granted by the third 'Volkskongress' (People's Congress) in May 1949 to a constitution first drafted by its offspring, the 'Volksrat' (People's Council) in October 1948.[14]

The whole Volkskongress movement, which had been spon-sored by the S.E.D. since late 1947 as representative of opinion

[13] Wolfgang Leonhard, *op. cit.*, p. 394.
[14] Boris Meissner, *Russland, die Westmächte und Deutschland* (Hamburg 1954), pp. 187, 213.

from all Germany, served in fact as the basis for the parliamentary half of the new state. The Volksrat, which had been delegated interim powers by the larger parental body simply met on October 7 and voted itself a 'Provisional People's Chamber' (Provisorische Volkskammer) on the basis of the previously-approved constitution. Without even bothering with the formality of elections to the legislature, either by the population directly or by the provincial legislatures, the new government was thus constituted as representative of the zone. The German Economic Commission (Deutsche Wirtschaftkommission—D.W.K.)—the central body hitherto responsible for the co-ordinated administration of zonal affairs—was turned overnight into the executive arm of the government. Former departments became governmental ministries charged with carrying out the enhanced administrative tasks passed to them through the dissolution of the Soviet Military Administration. This body was replaced in November by a Soviet Control Commission responsible for exercising the sovereign powers and fulfilling the obligations derived from Potsdam and other four-power agreements. Notwithstanding its wider responsibilities, the 'D.D.R.' in operation continued to be what its component parts had been before it—an administrative arm of the occupying power.

The chain of reactions between the Soviet policy of tying its zone ever more tightly into its Eastern orbit and the consequent Allied policy of resurrecting a strong Western Germany bound to the West European community—all within the increasing tensions of the world-wide Cold War—heightened antagonisms and deepened the divisions between the two parts of Germany. Nevertheless, the constant Soviet call for a return to the Potsdam Agreements in order to forestall the rehabilitation of the Western parts of the country, together with recurrent efforts to enlist German 'bourgeois nationalist' sentiment behind the drive for a 'neutralized' united Germany, had forestalled the outright revolutionizing of zonal society that would lead to the irreparable division of the country. Communications and trade between the zones were maintained, although with increasing restrictions; private ownership of property and of industry, though curtailed, was not eradicated; the middle class was not abolished; and agriculture was still totally in the hands of private peasants—in a word, Communist political domination, imposed from without, was saddled on a modified version of the economic and social structure that had existed before 1945.

The intensification of the Cold War following the outbreak

of the Korean War in June 1950 changed the situation. The obvious similarity between the exposed flank in Western Germany and that currently under attack in the East led the Western powers to accelerate the mobilization of their European defences. The rapid arming of the members of the North Atlantic Treaty Organization was begun, and it was decided that German military units must be organized to counter any possible invasion from the East. There ensued almost two years of prolonged negotiation within the Western bloc to reach agreement on what form this German contribution should take. Finally, it was agreed to integrate the German troops among the military units of the European members of N.A.T.O. —all subordinate to the Supreme Headquarters of the overall N.A.T.O. command; on May 27, 1952, the treaty establishing the European Defence Community was signed in Paris. The Bonn government, which simultaneously received almost full sovereignty, thereby tied itself even more strongly to the fortunes of the West.

Throughout this period the Communists carried on an especially vigorous propaganda campaign against the re-establishment of German military forces. Both in Germany and Western Europe generally the local Communists ably seconded the Soviet appeals to genuine fear regarding the revival of German militarism; however, particularly in Germany, there was an all-out attempt to capture nationalist and neutralist sentiment. The Communists warned that the erection of the E.D.C. would be the ultimate violation of the Potsdam Agreement and would lead to the irrevocable division of Germany. There could be no question of unity once half of the country had opted so fully for the Western Alliance. In this case, the Russians were as good as their word, for immediately after the signing of the Paris Treaty they proceeded to carry out their threats. The radical elements of the S.E.D. under the leadership of Ulbricht were given full sway, and the complete sovietization of the zone was begun.

In a four-hour report to the Second S.E.D. Party Conference in July 1952, Ulbricht announced the decision to proceed with the rapid 'building of the bases of socialism'. This amounted to the nationalization of all industry, a concentration on the expansion of heavy industry, the building and equipping of a zonal army, and the rapid collectivization of agriculture. Already at the end of May, a strengthening of the central governmental structure had begun, in order to bring it into conformity with that existing in the Soviet Union. Ulbricht emphasized in his report that this powerful state apparatus, based on a new legal system of 'socialist right', would be the chief instrument in the struggle against the 'great capitalists' and 'great farmers'. In June, Minister of State Security Zaisser had been ordered by President Pieck to take measures to seal off the zonal frontiers; Ulbricht followed this up in his report with an official call for the establishment of 'national military forces' for the protection of home and socialist successes in the zone. This new 'hard' line was further implemented when the government in July decreed the abolition of the five zonal länder; they were replaced with fifteen districts (kreise) administered from the centre. At the same time, the government assured itself of the necessary labour for industry by setting up a compulsory 'Dienst für Deutschland' (Service for Germany), much like the former 'Arbeitsdienst' of Hitler's Germany, but now modelled on the 'state labour reserves' system of the Soviet Union.[15]

As the campaign progressed, it became increasingly radical. By the spring of 1953 'intensified class warfare' was in full swing. On May 5, Ulbricht delivered a most uncompromising speech which illuminated the ideological aims involved and their implications for all of Germany. While bitterly attacking the West German 'bourgeois' parties, he characterized the East German state as 'successfully discharging the functions of a dictatorship of the proletariat', and maintained that reunification was only possible by extending this socialist revolution to Western Germany.[16] 'The building of socialism' in effect meant the building of an independent source of power in East Germany; and with its summary abandonment in June 1953 one finds the Soviet zone leaders admitting as much through their criticism of it. After the riots of June 16-17, this criticism and self-criticism took on an added urgency through the increased pressure exerted from above by the Soviet authorities and from below by the discontented population. Seldom is it possible to gain such frank and official admissions of Communist intentions and their failure.

In a speech to a group of workers in Boehlen on June 24, 1953 —a week after the riots and almost two weeks after the introduction of the 'New Course'—Premier of the 'German Democratic Republic' Otto Grotewohl set forth what he branded the 'twin mistakes' of 'rapidly building socialism':

[15] For a summary of all these East German measures in May-July 1952, together with detailed documentation, see Boris Meissner, *op. cit.*, pp. 308-15.

[16] British Broadcasting Corporation, *Summary of World Broadcasts*, Pt. III, Germany and Austria, No. 208, pp. 2-9.

We mistakenly believed that our economic development had advanced much further than was actually the case. When, last summer, we started to expand our heavy industry as an important preliminary to establishing better living conditions, we overlooked two things. We ignored the fact that there was no need at all to build up a heavy industry on the scale planned, if we concentrated all efforts of the German working class and the Republic on the achievement of German unity. We thought the question of German unity so remote that we must try to get straight by our own efforts.

He then went on to admit that if German unity were the cardinal aim of policy, all efforts must be directed toward bringing the Eastern and Western parts together. The old policy had endangered this goal, for it was driving divisions between Germany. 'People were becoming estranged.'[17]

Tangible proof of this estrangement is contained in the statistics on the steadily increasing number of East Germans who were fleeing West. In December 1952 9,543 former inhabitants of East Germany applied for permission to resettle in the Federal Republic; in March 1953 the number had climbed to 51,359. In the first week of June alone the number was 39,091.[18] A refugee who fled the zone after the riots described the conditions which gave rise to these statistics:

We hadn't seen butter, margarine, or any other fats for months. Potatoes, as you know, mean to the German what spaghetti means to an Italian. Well, potatoes were first rationed and then disappeared entirely. In recent months, there had been less food than ever. Whole villages had been abandoned. The farmers were afraid of collectivization, and ran off to Western Germany, leaving their fields to go to seed. . . . Our bread became dark and very expensive. Bakers were forbidden to tell their customers what they put into the bread. The price of everything was going up all the time. The distribution system had broken down. . . . There was a widespread feeling that life simply could not go on like that much longer.[19]

[17] British Broadcasting Corporation, *op. cit.*, No. 215, p. 4.

[18] These figures, together with additional ones for the intervening months, are quoted by Theodore Lit, 'The Proletariat vs. The Dictatorship', *Problems of Communism*, Vol. II, No. 6, 1953, p. 3. See also: *Der Aufstand im Juni, Ein Dokument-arischer Bericht* (Berlin 1954), p. 7. This report first appeared in *Der Monat*, Heft 60 and 61 (September and October 1953).

[19] Joseph Wechsberg, 'A Reporter in Germany—the Seventeenth of June' *The New Yorker*, August 29, 1953, p. 34.

The tensions caused between the two halves of Germany by this inflexible policy, not to speak of its economic failure, did not fit Soviet policy as it developed after the death of Stalin. Coexistence and relaxation of tension in Europe could mean nothing so long as this policy of active hostility toward and separation from Western Germany was continued. It not only alienated German opinion, but it prevented any talk with the Western powers about German unification. *Pravda* on May 24, 1953, printed a leading editorial in answer to Churchill's speech in the House of Commons on May 11. While restating the Soviet desire for peaceful coexistence and praising Churchill's initiative in proposing a meeting at the summit, a long section dealt with the German question. The Soviet government agreed with Churchill that it was 'the paramount problem of Europe' and that its settlement would aid greatly in easing international tension. As was to be expected, the editorial criticized sharply British policy in Western Germany, and denied accusations regarding the state of affairs in Eastern Germany. However, it resurrected the old Soviet line that agreement in Germany must be based on the wartime accords reached at Yalta and Potsdam. It is worth noting that the policy then being carried on in Eastern Germany was diametrically opposite to one of the major provisions of Potsdam—that Germany should be treated as an economic and political unity. If the new Soviet government wished to use the Potsdam formula as a possible basis for drawing the West into discussions over Germany, they certainly must take action in their zone to ease the situation in a rapidly dividing Germany.

The answer was the 'New Course' pronouncements which came suddenly with no outside warning. West German sources have since produced reports, hard to substantiate, that the Soviet government had dispatched a note to the Central Committee of the Socialist Unity Party as early as April 16, 1953, which proposed a reversal of the rigorous policy. It is maintained that the S.E.D. was reluctant to do this sharply, preferring instead 'to build down to it slowly'. This line, therefore, maintains that the possibility of sharp reversal was actually discussed and dismissed by the East German Communists in April and May, only to be forced upon them by the Russians in June.[20] There is some slight evidence to support the contention that the change had been previously discussed among the German hierarchy. On June 27, 1953, Wilhelm Pieck, President

[20] 'Das Dilemma der S.E.D.', *S.B.Z. Archiv, Dokumente, Berichte, Kommentare—zu gesamtdeutschen Fragen*, July 5, 1953, p. 200.

of the Republic, signed a telegram for popular circulation which gave his full support for the new concessionary measures being enacted during his sick leave in the Soviet Union. He added by way of explanation that he had given his full support to the proposed change when it had been discussed with him by Politbureau representatives before its enactment on June 9.[21] Whether or not this is true and there was any discussion in Party councils about a possible change, the fact remains that there was absolutely no concrete intimation of its impending enactment. The harsh policy of 'rapidly building the bases of socialism' was the mainstay of East German policy up to the sudden reversal on June 9.

Furthermore, Soviet actions immediately preceding the pronouncements point to the conclusion that they were suddenly imposed from Moscow. On May 28 the Kremlin announced that the military Control Commission in Berlin was being dissolved and that Semyonov, former political adviser to the Commission, was replacing it as Soviet High Commissioner for Germany. This move brought the Soviet organization technically in line with the position the Western envoys had enjoyed in their part of Germany for the past two years. Semyonov had previously been recalled to Moscow from Berlin on April 22, 1953, but his departure had found no apparent reflection in a changed Soviet or East German policy. In retrospect, it seems probable that he had been recalled to Moscow for consultation on the projected change in Germany; four days after his return to Berlin on June 5, the dramatic reversal occurred.

This reversal came in the form of a communiqué from the S.E.D. Politbureau. The first paragraph set out what was to be accomplished and how, as well as intimating just how critical the condition was:

> The Politbureau of the S.E.D. Central Committee decided at its meeting on June 9, 1953, to recommend to the government of the German Democratic Republic a number of measures which will contribute to a marked improvement in the standard of living of all sections of the population, and which will strengthen the certainty of law (Rechtssicherheit) in the Republic. The Politbureau based its decision on the fact that a number of mistakes have been made in the past by both the S.E.D. and the government, mistakes reflected in ordinances such as those on the reorganization of the

[21] British Broadcasting Corporation, *op. cit.*, p. 14. These remarks are reiterated in an article which Pieck wrote for *Neues Deutschland* and *Taegliche Rundschau*, July 2, 1953.

ration card system, on the taking over of derelict agricultural holdings, on special measures for the collection of (agricultural) deliveries, on more drastic methods of tax collection, and others.[22]

There was to be a return to legality, and special interests of the middle class—the private peasants, retail traders, craftsmen and non-Communist intelligentsia—were to be bolstered. This was the class that was being forced out of existence under the old policy—the decision in April to withdraw ration books of the middle class in the cities having been but a thinly disguised attempt to starve them into submission. The Politbureau communiqué further announced that the plan for heavy industry must be curtailed so as to increase the amount of consumers' goods available. There was a determined bid to get back as many of the defectors as possible, for it was also promised that all those who returned would either receive compensation or restitution of property previously confiscated. There was a specific reference to lenient handling of farmers who returned to take up their old land, another indication of how many of those fleeing West had come from the countryside. The drive against recalcitrant students and teachers was halted; peace with the Church was to be negotiated; price increases in sugar products dating from April 1953 were rescinded; and all political prisoners serving one to three years imprisonment or who were in the process of being prosecuted were to be released. In a word, the stringent policy of the past ten months was to be abandoned and reversed.

The aim of this change was quite clearly stated in the communiqué:

> In making this decision the Politbureau has as its great aim the restoration of the unity of Germany, which requires of both sides measures which will really facilitate the coming together of the two parts of Germany.[23]

Immediate moves along these lines were instituted with the easing of travel restrictions between the two zones, and the granting of visas for scientists, artists, etc., to visit Western Germany. It was also stated that Western Germans would now be able to visit their relatives in Eastern Germany. On June 16,

[22] *Neues Deutschland*, organ of the Central Committee of the S.E.D., June 11, 1953. The text of the communiqué is printed in full by Bundesministerium für gesamtdeutsche Fragen, *Der Volksaufstand vom 17. Juni 1953, Denkschrift über den Juni-Aufstand in der Sovjetischen Besatzungszone und in Ostberlin* (Bonn 1953), Doc. 18, p. 35.   [23] *Ibid.*

Grotewohl underlined this reversal on German unification in his speech to the Parteiaktiv meeting in Berlin. After admitting that the old policy had led to a widening of the gulf between Western and Eastern Germany—'an intolerable state of affairs' —he drew the necessary conclusions:

> Our Party and government are carrying out a change of course which is essential for speedily raising the people's living standard and bringing about the necessary understanding among Germans.[24]

This one sentence states quite succinctly that essential connection between internal development and external affairs which underlay the 'New Course' reversals.

This unprepared change was a staggering blow to the Party. It called for a complete reorientation, an absolute reversal of tactics and aims. Those elements which were enemies yesterday were to be strengthened to-day. It put an intolerable strain on the whole structure of a regime already weakened by the Draconic measures it had forced on an unwilling population. That population was now asked to believe that in the space of one day there had been a complete change of heart, that a new and better policy could be carried out by that government which had pursued the ruinous policy of the past. Grovelling self-criticism accompanying great concessions to the people— both obviously imposed from without—was supposed to wipe out overnight the bitterness of the past.

In the very suddenness of their reversal, the Communist regime made the fatal mistake of ignoring that class upon which they were most dependent—the workers. Though weakened by the lack of faith the Soviets had shown in them and their old policy, the S.E.D. still attempted to compel a raising of the working norms by 10%.

II

Though the June 9 Politbureau decision had referred to measures aimed at helping 'workers, peasants, intelligentsia, artisans and other sections of the middle class', neither this communiqué nor the government's decision officially implementing it on June 11 contained any direct concessions to the workers as a separate group. No mention was made of rescinding the Council of Ministers' decision of May 28, 1953, which had ordered the 10% raising of all working norms by June 30. Under the circumstances, its attempted implementation after

[24] British Broadcasting Corporation, *op. cit.*, No. 214, p. 23.

the announcement of the 'New Course' was to have disastrous effects for the government, since here may be found the immediate cause of the mass demonstrations which engulfed Berlin beginning on June 16.

The decree of May 28, 'complying with the request for a general revision and raising of the work norms expressed by wide circles of the working people',[25] was merely the culmination of an ever-intensified campaign among the workers begun in the early months of 1953. A pertinent sentence in a S.E.D. Central Committee decision of February 3 had set the theme: 'For the productive exploitation of the work day and the increase of work productivity, technically justified, progressive work norms are to be introduced; the struggle for the increase of norms is to be organized.' In numerous articles and Party pronouncements thereafter, it was stressed that the wage structure did not correspond to overall production results, that individual production norms were being fulfilled while general plans went unfulfilled. An article in *Neues Deutschland* of March 5 outlined what this meant specifically, by using the Steel and Rolling Mill at Groeditz as a case in point. It began by stating that 'the meaning of the regime of thrift and the principle of efficiency is still underrated by workers and management', and drew examples from a hypothetical brigade of ten workers. The writer showed that while the whole production norm of this team of men was just fulfilled—i.e. total achievement was 100%, the work being finished only in the scheduled time—the wages each of the men was paid varied anywhere from 113% to 140% of individual norm fulfilment. The conclusion followed naturally: 'Obviously there is a miscalculation of the process of work, for the amount of wages distributed does not correspond to the overall fulfilment of the norm.'[26]

In a two-page article in *Neues Deutschland* on April 16, Walter Ulbricht gave the rationale for the whole movement to establish 'technically-sound' norms. First, he reiterated that the 'laying of the foundations of socialism' meant the reconstruction of existing enterprises on socialist lines. Then—

> In accordance with the law of extended reproduction of the socialist economy, we must concentrate chiefly on the development of the heavy and machine-building industries, thus paving the way for a higher standard of living. The fundamental problem is to achieve a constant increase in labour productivity and a constant cut in production costs.

[25] Bundesministerium für Gesamtdeutsche Fragen, *op. cit.*, Doc. 17, p. 34.
[26] *Id.*, Doc. 2, p. 18.

... We realize that the technical basis of production in most branches of our economy is obsolete and that we must make a greater effort to modernize our enterprises and make them technically perfect.

A few paragraphs later he applied the above to the problem of working norms:

Norms which have long ago become obsolete as a result of technical progress and the better organization of work serve in many places as a basis for calculating wages which are so high that they no longer offer any incentive for technical improvements, better organization of work and reduction in costs. The lack of technically sound norms and the failure to fix new norms every year is an obstacle to the growth of socialism.[27]

The problem of the working norms is seen to be at base the problem of increasing production in an economy of austerity which is attempting to 'build socialism'. 'Technically-based' norms meant those that effectively compel a constant rise in worker productivity—in the words of Stalin quoted in the above-quoted article by Ulbricht—those that 'constitute a great regulating force which ranges the broad masses of industrial workers around the advanced elements of the working class'.

In simple practical terms, the imperative behind this drive was the galloping inflation in the zone. Not only was industry severely dislocated by its rapid reorganization and socialization, but there was also an overwhelming stress on heavy industry to the detriment of consumer goods industry. The largest section of the population—the workers—were being paid money wages out of all proportion to actual production; at the same time what was produced did not satisfy either their needs or the needs of the peasantry. There was no incentive for increased agricultural production, a production which was already falling sharply due to the drastic collectivization of the peasantry simultaneously with the socialization of industry. There was money but no goods—a classic inflationary situation.

This connection between dire conditions in supply and excessive wages was underlined by an official of the Ministry of Finance before a meeting of the Greater Berlin S.E.D. Party Cabinet on June 4. He stated that correct price calculations for goods depended in turn on a correct calculation of the 'necessary social outlay' on labour and means of production. Such

[27] This whole article was broadcast over the East German radio and is reproduced in *id.*, No. 205, pp. 24-5.

outlay largely depended upon the actions of the workers, that is, a lowering of production costs through higher labour productivity and better utilization of the means of production. He concluded that the disturbance causing the government 'the greatest concern' was the excess purchasing power which caused a constant upward pressure in prices of consumer goods.[28]

The obvious solution was to cut down the purchasing power of the worker, and this could best be achieved by an increase in production without a corresponding increase in wages. In practice, it meant increasing the working norms, and the S.E.D. had set out to do just that. The original aim was to persuade the workers in each factory to accept raised norms as part of an improved organization of production. If the two went hand-in-hand, theoretically there would be no reduction in wages or added hardships. The drive was coupled with an appeal to loyalty toward the republic, and invoked the argument of all Communist regimes—that increased production and possible temporary sacrifices now are necessary to the 'creation of socialism', and hence to a better life in the future. Though unofficial, the campaign was to be comprehensive, as the Party network spread throughout the whole zone. Norm revisions would start simultaneously in each individual factory and would spread outwards and upwards through each industry and ministry. If this had been successful, any governmental decree would simply establish as law a condition which already existed generally.

Throughout the first half of 1953 there was unrelenting stress on the duty of the S.E.D. party organizations to organize the actions of the workers. An article in the *Sächsische Zeitung* of April 14 described the general tasks of the lower party organizations:

> The most important basic organizations of our Party are the Party organizations in the factories. Above all they have the tasks to convince the workers of the correctness of the policy of our Party and of our government, and to mobilize them for the realization of the tasks given them by the Second Party Conference. But this leading role of the Party is safeguarded only if the decisions of the higher committees are conscientiously carried out.[29]

Ulbricht's *Neues Deutschland* article of April 16 fitted this role of the basic Party organization into the implementation of the higher Party decision to raise the norms:

[28] British Broadcasting Corporation, *op. cit.*, No. 212, pp. 9-10.
[29] Ministerium für Gesamtdeutsche Fragen, *op. cit.*, Doc. 3, pp. 18-19.

The Party trade union organization in every enterprise must conduct systematic enlightenment work on the importance of technically sound norms. The foremen in many factory departments, helped by the workers and engineering staff, work out such norms and thereby raise output. The norms are then introduced on the management's instructions.

He made it quite clear that the ultimate responsibility belonged to the hierarchy of the factory management, whose duty was constantly to improve the organization of work, thereby lowering production costs.

The ultimate inability of the Socialist Unity Party to carry through the norm revision without resorting to the legal sanction of a governmental decree demonstrates its loose and poor organization in the factories. This failure gives a necessary insight into conditions preparatory to the riots of June 16 and 17. Numerous articles in the Party press during the first six months of 1953 pointed out that not only was there no connection between the basic Party organizations and the 'broad masses of the working population', but also liaison between these organizations and the central Party organizations in the hierarchy above them—from the central factory committee to the Kreis (Area) and Bezirk (Regional) Committees—was lacking. An article entitled 'Only the Close Connection with the Masses Safeguards the Leading Role of the Party' in the S.E.D. periodical *Neuer Weg*, February 1953, attacked the central Party organization in the Ernst Thaelmann Works, Magdeburg, for shirking its responsibilities in mobilizing both the basic factory organizations and the workers. The organization was pictured as lying under the tutelage of the factory management, which fact hampered its becoming the leading force in the works. There was no intra-committee discussion and the Committee itself failed to act on suggestions made to it by the basic organizations. Furthermore, a Party Aktiv meeting of representatives from the Bezirk and Kreis Committees and qualified instructors from the economic administration had discovered that a number of 'Party enemies' had infiltrated the individual basic organizations. These had exploited levelling tendencies among the workers, i.e. a desire to cut down the great differential in bonuses and wages paid to various categories of workers. In addition, functionaries and Party members, frustrated or punished by the Party, had lodged themselves in the works, with the following consequences:

We failed to observe these comrades afterwards, and to-day the state of affairs in our works (Ernst Thaelmann) is such that many of those punished have flocked together with evil Social Democrats, formed groups and cliques there and thus engaged, in the interests of the enemy, in provocations, which eventually could end up in these hostile activities in December.

'These hostile activities' turned out to be work stoppages in connection with the distribution of end-of-the-year bonuses, and they took place not only in the Ernst Thaelmann Works, but 'in all Magdeburg'.[30] This admission of work stoppages in connection with a break in the Party structure as early as December 1952 is highly significant, especially in light of the similar explanations given after the June uprising some seven months later.

The press unremittently attacked lower officials for hampering progress in the revision of norms. For example, an article in *Neues Deutschland* of March 5, 1953, criticized the secretaries of the Party and local trade union in the Groeditz Steel and Rolling Mill for holding the opinion 'that the development of the workers' consciousness has not yet proceeded so far that one can frankly discuss an alteration with them'.[31] An article in *Neues Deutschland* on March 28 struck the same theme:

> As most managements and trade union officials, filled with an opportunist lack of faith in the working masses, have steered clear of the supposed hot iron of norm increases, the production workers, aware of their responsibility as masters of the undertakings and of production, have themselves undertaken the first decisive step by raising their own norms.

It ended by calling for a revision in every factory 'without waiting for an ordinance to this effect', and stated that the Party organizations must concentrate on norm raising.[32] Of course, the real problem was the reluctance of the workers to take a cut in wages, and the ineffectualness of the Party supporters only reflected it. An article in *Neues Deutschland* on April 22 stated this quite forthrightly, using the 'Karl Marx' Works in Berlin as a case in point. The workers there had stated 'they were not so mad as to raise their norms voluntarily', for they wanted to earn money. The Party organization was still to blame for this state of affairs, for they had failed to teach the various departments in the plant how to organize their work

[30] This article is reprinted in full in *id.*, Doc. 1, pp. 17-18.
[31] *Id.*, Doc. 2, p. 18.   [32] *Id.*, Doc. 5, p. 20.

properly, so as to be able to introduce raised norms without a concomitant reduction in wages.

A good part of the thirteenth session of the S.E.D. Central Committee meeting on May 13 and 14 dealt with this flagging campaign; in the end, it pointed the way to the final governmental decision two weeks later. Deputy Premier Henrich Rau, during a long and not very encouraging report on the condition of industry, called for a 'fundamental change' in industrial activity if the construction of the bases of socialism was to be achieved. After noting that the gross production for industry had been fulfilled by 103·4% in 1952, he admitted that several of the most important items—electric power, rolling mill and other metallurgical equipment—lagged behind. This was especially true of investment plans in these areas; for example, the investment plan for an increase in the generating capacity of the electric power industry was fulfilled by only 46%, in the case of rolling mills material—19%, of steel—73%, of cement —75%. These failures in heavy industrial investment affected all branches of the economy. Furthermore, and most important, the level of industrial production reached during the fourth quarter of 1952 had not been maintained during the first quarter of 1953. It had dropped by 10%, with the result that plan fulfilment for this quarter in industrial production had been only 96·2%.[33]

He went on to say that technological development in the two-year Reconstruction Plan of 1948-50, and the first two years of the present five-year plan (1950-55) had progressed rapidly, as had the skilled training of the workers. The present tasks of the five-year plan could only be fulfilled by raising labour productivity to match this previous progress, and the key to this was the fixing of correct technical norms. This question had not received enough attention, since in comparison with the total number of norms those fixed through practical experience only amounted to 62·8%. Fortunately, the workers' 'high degree of class consciousness' had manifested itself in a development of a movement for the examination of existing working norms. This 'norm review' movement had become so great that the Party must put it on a more organized footing. Party and trade union organizations must provide the leadership for the movement; at the same time, the isolation of the Party Organizations in the factory from Kreis (area) and Bezirk (district) executives must end.[34]

Rau followed with a concrete proposal which was a departure

[33] British Broadcasting Corporation, *op. cit.*, No. 209, pp. 4-8.   [34] *Id.*, pp. 8-21.

from all past pronouncements in the campaign. The Politbureau had decided to call for the general raising of all norms by 10% immediately, in order to achieve quick results. Technically-sound norms could be established once the effects of this rise had been evaluated. He saw this as the only way to get around the discrepancy between individual norm fulfilment and general plan fulfilment.

Here was the first mention of any general raising of norms by administrative action; it was the origin of the policy pursued by the government during the first week in June. The Polit-bureau had switched to a new front, since the lower organizations had been unable to implement its decisions through persuasion from the ground up. True, the action was to be preliminary to the fixing of technical norms through the co-operative evaluation of the results of the increase in each enterprise by the S.E.D. factory organization, works trade union committee, management, and labour department. Nevertheless, the rise was to come first from above, and in the face of past opposition among the workers to any increase in their working quotas.

The Central Committee Resolution of May 13-14, concerning the 'Raising of Work Productivity and the Carrying Through of the Strictest Saving', merely filled in the details. Work norms were to be raised 10% by June 1, and were to be valid at least until December 31. Between these two dates a general study of the norms was to be undertaken in the manner outlined in Rau's speech. In this way, it would be able to have at least 50% of the most important norms technically based by January 1, 1954. Meanwhile, the factory Party organizations and the trade unions were to explain to the workers the meaning of the work norms and 'the necessity for their yearly revision and raising'. Two key sections of the resolution are worth quoting, for they show how the immediate revision was to be implemented from above. The Central Committee resolved:

1. That the responsible officials of the ministries and the State Secretariats for each branch of industry, for each factory and for each department should lay down key figures for an increase of labour norms, and that this should be done in such a fashion as to obtain a general increase of labour norms by at least 10%.

2. The Works Manager should confirm the working norms increased in this fashion and make them known in writing to the staff before their introduction.[35]

35 Bundesministerium für Gesamtdeutsche Fragen, *op. cit.*, Doc. 15, p. 32.

The government Decree of May 28 followed this resolution almost word for word, and did little more than give it formal legality. A few more details were added and the deadline of June 1 for introduction of the first revision was forwarded to June 30, but the aim remained the same.

One source has estimated the loss accruing to various types of workers. A bricklayer would lose roughly 30% of his pay, a carpenter even up to 42%. A construction worker would now receive only 13 to 16 DM. (East) a day compared to his previous 20 to 24 DM. (East).[36] During the first week of June the East German radio continued with its usual volume of reports about voluntary increases in working norms; however, there were reports of a certain amount of opposition as well. For instance, A.D.N., the East German news agency, reported that all the workers at the heavy machine works 'Karl Liebknecht' in Magdeburg had not immediately agreed to the increase. A blacksmith was singled out as refusing until his colleagues convinced him that a norm increase did not mean a lowering of real wages. Another time *Neues Deutschland* in its issue of June 2, 1953, admitted that the higher norms would at first mean a temporary decline in workers' wages. However, once the production increases caused by the new norms had been put into operation generally, prices would soon fall and balance would be restored.[37]

A long *Neues Deutschland* leader of June 14 by Siegfried Gruen and Kaethe Stern, entitled 'Es Wird Zeit, den Holzhammer Beiseite zu Legen' (It is Time to Put Aside the Wooden Hammer),[38] is of paramount importance, for it centres on the attempts to introduce the new norms in the construction sites in Berlin. The time and place are extremely significant: It is only five days after the original announcement of the New Course and two days before the beginning of the disturbances on June 16; the place is the Stalinallee Construction sites, the starting point of the uprising. The article breathes that new tone of self-critical weakness assumed by the Party after the New Course pronouncement; at the same time, it gives indisputable proof of the seething resentment of the workers about the continued attempts to force through a raising of their working norms. These two factors—the sudden weakening of

---

[36] Research and Library Unit, Munich Radio Centre, *The Rebellion of June 17, 1953* (Munich 1954), p. 14. This is an unpublished report put out by the United States Information Service, Voice of America.

[37] British Broadcasting Corporation, *op. cit.*, No. 212, p. 13.

[38] Reproduced in full by Bundesministerium für Gesamtdeutsche Fragen, *op. cit.*, Doc. 23, pp. 41-3.

the Party's position and the desperate mood of the workers—
were to combine in an explosion that rocked the zone. With
astonishing clarity the official East German press has demonstrated just how critical conditions were, and how little hold
the Party had over these workers. With the vision of hindsight,
one can see how the strikes and uprising to which they gave
birth could develop naturally out of the atmosphere of active
discontent so forthrightly portrayed here.

The article begins with a long exposition of what 'voluntarily
raised norms' had meant on one building site in Berlin—at the
V.E.B. (People's Owned Works) 'Wohnungsbau'. On May 1
it had been said that 125 brigades had already raised their
norms there. Yet on May 28 a meeting took place to discuss a
general raising of the norms by 10% for the whole enterprise,
with the result that the majority decided against the proposal.
The obvious conclusion is drawn: The original claim about
voluntarily raised norms must have been fabricated. The article
continues:

> At about the same time (i.e. May 28) there came the
> alarming news from Section G—North in Stalinallee that some
> brigades (work teams), owing to differences with the norm-
> ing department, had not resumed work in the morning. At
> Strausberger Platz (in the middle of the Stalinallee) similar
> events took place, where carpenter brigades of the V.E.B.
> Wohnungsbau are working.
>
> One should have thought that these signs of dissatisfaction
> among the workers ought to have been a stimulus for the
> factory management and the Party committee to review
> critically their work and also the previous news on the raising
> of the norms by 125 brigades.[39]

Instead of taking heed, the Party Secretary, Müller, stood behind the norming department and blamed the trouble on one
man—the head of a brigade, Rocke. The authors then show
the misdirection of this judgment regarding an exemplary
worker, and in so doing illuminate the nefarious methods that
had been used in raising norms 'voluntarily'. At the beginning
of May, Rocke was first told lies by the norm expert and other
members of the management about his colleagues already
having agreed to raise their norms. Then, in Rocke's own
words:

> When this manoeuvre did not work with me, Leinbeck
> (the management's norm expert) told me that I ought to

[39] *Id.*, p. 41.

know that they would let work on the big construction sites only such brigades as had raised their norms. Thereupon we increased our norms by an average of 6·5 per cent. But in my eyes that was sheer blackmail.[40]

The article brings out the psychology of the workers quite lucidly. At one point, the writers are told: 'You do not dare, after all, to write in the newspaper what we are going to tell you.' Another time, the workers are quoted as saying: 'You must understand us after all. We work and we are willing to build. We are only so excited because the work in the firm management is not all right.'[41] This section concludes with a clear warning to the norm experts and management:

> If the norm experts believe that they can make their reputation at the firm management by their dangerous trick, they are mistaken. For they have the construction workers against them, without whom the firm can never function smoothly. . . . The norm experts must be helpers to the brigades and together with them carry through the assessment of progressive norms.[42]

There follows in the last section a scathing indictment of the Party Secretary, Müller, for his lack of understanding, self-conceit, for his 'smug and superior' behaviour. All this is put under a sub-heading, 'The Dictators'. A quotation from the lower Party Secretary at one of the construction sites suffices to show the condition of organization between lower and higher party units:

> Comrade Müller is uncritical towards his own work. He has forgotten that we have a Party organization of our own on the building site. That is why he never discusses anything with me. He arrives without our knowing anything about it and creates unrest by his way of discussing with the construction workers. . . . By discussions as he leads them, he does not help, but destroys the confidence of the workers in the Party.[43]

This 'bad example' of Müller and the whole Bezirk (Area) Committee of Greater Berlin in roughly enforcing working discipline cannot be tolerated. It abuses the workers' trust, something they cannot be expected to accept.[44] The conclusion regarding the introduction of new norms is extremely significant:

> The Party organization of the V.E.B. Wohungsbau must see to it that the decisions of our government and Party are

[40] *Ibid.*   [41] *Id.*, p. 42.   [42] *Ibid.*   [43] *Ibid.*   [44] *Id.*, p. 43.

not carried out in an authoritarian and administrative fashion. A raising of the norms cannot be declared binding for a brigade before the members of the brigade have been convinced of the importance of these measures for our struggle for a better life. Any other way to the raising of the norms will have negative effects for the firm. The most dangerous thing in this connection is that by authoritarian and administrative introduction of measures we shall repel our workers from us instead of binding them closer and closer to us.[45]

Here, just two days before the beginning of the events which were to show so dramatically how much the workers were 'repelled', is sufficient proof that the danger was realized. It also shows the dilemma of the authorities: they desperately needed the raised norms to increase production for a 'better life'; at the same time they ran the great risk of alienating the workers completely by forcing their introduction. If the lessons outlined in the above quotation could have been applied, the strikes of June 16 and hence the rising of June 17 might have been avoided. However, as will be shown, they were not—and indeed could not—be applied. For, in effect, these lessons contradicted the whole spirit of the May 28 decree and the Central Committee resolution preceding it. Furthermore, it was illusory to expect that the behaviour of the whole Party hierarchy—so clearly outlined in this article—could change overnight, especially when it was the approach and not the policy regarding the norms that was to be changed.

Direct testimony of construction workers on Stalinallee further proves that after the New Course pronouncements, the opposition to the new norms mounted steadily to a crescendo. One man reports that on Friday June 12 at Building site C—South in Stalinallee the workmen were called together by the foreman at midday and read the following statement: 'After full discussion on the building sites, the men are prepared to raise their norms by an average of 10%.' 250 workers threw down their tools and refused to work until the decision was revoked. About 2.30, fifteen functionaries of the Party management and the trade union arrived, and tried to split up the recalcitrant workers into small discussion groups. This was a recurring tactic in the following days: to break the opposition by dividing it. After much argument, it was finally agreed to hold a meeting of the whole construction site on the next morning, Saturday June 13, at 11.00. However, when the

[45] *Ibid.*

workers arrived back early that morning, they found thirty functionaries waiting and ready to discuss with them in small groups. In attempting to effect a resumption of work, the functionaries swore that the workers on the other construction sites had given their consent to the government decisions on the norms. Though they did not achieve this object—so busy was everyone discussing, they did succeed in dispensing with the planned general meeting.[46]

That Saturday afternoon seems to have been a crucial time in the movement toward the strikes of June 16. An outing was held on the Muggelsee at Ruebezahl to which all workers belonging to the huge state undertaking 'V.E.B. Industriebau' were admitted, upon payment of 3 DM. (East). There were numerous co-workers of other unions present, among them workers from Bloc 40 in the Stalinallee.[47] In this way, workers from many of the different construction sites had a chance to communicate their mutual grievances to one another and to feel their united opposition. All reports agree that the increased norms were the major topic of conversation during the day. The first payments on the basis of the new norms had already been made that past week in some enterprises and the workers were incensed. On the steamer trip back from the outing, some who had drunk a good deal had particularly violent discussions with members of the S.E.D. For the first time, the word 'Generalstreik' was heard.[48] One report states quite specifically that the workers from the building yard Friedrichsheim (East Berlin) decided that they would carry out a protest strike on Monday June 15 unless the decree of May 28 was withdrawn.[49]

On Sunday the long *Neues Deutschland* article outlined above appeared with its unusually conciliatory tone and suggestive title. Then on Monday June 15 a meeting of all the workers in Bloc 40 in Stalinallee was called by an S.E.D. functionary, in order to pass a resolution thanking Walter Ulbricht and Otto Grotewohl for their decisions of June 11. Someone from the floor suggested that a request for the lowering of the norms be included. After a debate it was voted to include this as a request, rather than a demand as some had wanted. The chairman of the trade union committee suggested waiting until a represent-

---

[46] Joachim G. Leithäuser (ed.), *Der Aufstand im Juni, Ein dokumentarischer Bericht* (Berlin 1954), pp. 11-12. This report first appeared in *Der Monat*, Heft 60 and 61 (September and October, 1953).   [47] *Id.*, p. 12.

[48] Joachim G. Leithäuser (ed.), *op. cit.*, p. 12, Also Stefan Brant, *Der Aufstand* (1954), p. 100.

[49] International Confederation of Free Trade Unions, *Workers' Fists Against Soviet Steel* (1953), p. 10.

ative had come to Stalinallee to discuss the norms question. However, Bloc 40 refused to wait and elected two delegates to take the resolution directly to Ulbricht and Grotewohl. When they were commanded to wait by the union committee, the workers refused to work until some satisfactory solution to the question of the norms had been reached. 'This downing of tools spread like wildfire down the Allee, but as working hours were almost over, no larger actions followed.'[50]

It can be seen from the above that the scene was set by June 16. The workers were becoming aggressive, while the Party and trade union functionaries were less and less able to restrain them. Their weakness and indecision in the face of the workers' hostility was manifest. All that was needed was a final blow to turn the open discontent of the workers into active hostility.

Such a blow fell on the morning of the 16th, with the publication of an article on the norms by Otto Lehmann, Secretary of the Central Committee of the F.D.G.B., in the trade union newspaper *Die Tribuene*.[51] This article not only rejected talk of doing away with the government Decree on raising the norms, but it also stated quite specifically that the New Course Pronouncements were in no way related to the norm increases:

> In connection with the publication of the communiqués of the Politbureau and the Council of Ministers on June 9 and 11 respectively, in several cases the question is raised as to how far the resolutions about the raising of the work norms are still correct, and how far they remain in effect. Indeed, the resolutions about the raising of the norms are correct to the fullest extent.

There followed a restatement of the government's aims in the New Course—to institute immediate measures to raise the standard of living of all parts of the population in Eastern Germany. It appeared that the workers were to bear the burden of these concessions to the population:

> Since, however, all that depends on how far we can obtain the great goals of the five-year plan on the basis of an established growth in workers' productivity through the strictest economy, it is valid to carry through with all our strength the resolution of the Council of Ministers regarding the raising of the work norms on the average of 10% by June 30, 1953.

Otto Nuschke, head of the C.D.U. in the zone and a Deputy

[50] Joachim G. Leithäuser (ed.), *op. cit.*, pp. 12-13.
[51] Reproduced in full by Bundesministerium für Gesamtdeutsche Fragen, *op. cit.*, Doc. 24, p. 43.

Premier in the 'National Front' government, later substantiated the major role of this article in initiating the disturbances. In the heat of uprising on June 17, Nuschke was pushed across into West Berlin. He was apprehended by the West Berlin police and taken to American headquarters, where later that day he gave a radio interview to R.I.A.S.—Radio in the American Sector. The following exchange occurred about his contention that the disturbances were not an outburst of popular discontent:

Question: How, then, do you account for the participation by the whole population in the Eastern zone?

Nuschke: Because *Tribuene*, the trade union paper, printed matter to the contrary.

Question: What did the paper say?

Nuschke: It said that the report (about rescinding the decree) was incorrect and that the higher norms remained in force.[52]

This attempt to present the belated reforms regarding the norms as a premeditated act is dubious, indeed, in light of the relative timing of Lehmann's article in *Tribuene* and the first government action contradicting it. The first Politbureau announcement came over the East Berlin radio at 3.30 p.m. on June 16,[53] well after the construction workers from Stalinallee had flooded through the centre of the city to the government buildings. It seems likely that the concessions contained in it were wrung from the government by the pressure of this mass strike. On the whole it cannot be said that the tone of the announcement was very conciliatory. It sounded more as though the Politbureau was abandoning its position with great reluctance. Only in the short second paragraph was the compulsory norm increase cancelled, with the proviso that the government decision of May 28 should be reviewed by the government jointly with the trade unions. The introductory paragraph put forth quite emphatically once again the Party's position on raised norms. They were absolutely necessary, but they must be put into effect voluntarily:

A new way of life can be built and the living conditions of workers and the population as a whole can be improved only by raising labour productivity and production. . . . The Politbureau is, therefore, of the opinion that the initiative of the most progressive workers in voluntarily raising their working norms is an important step on the road to building

[52] *Id.*, Doc. 25, p. 45. See also: British Broadcasting Corporation, *op. cit.*, No. 214, p. 18.

[53] British Broadcasting Corporation, *op. cit.*, No. 214, p. 2.

a new way of life—a step which shows the whole population the way out of existing difficulties.[54]

The Politbureau took the view that managers, trade unions, and Party organizations had the urgent task 'to improve working organization and production so that the wages of workers who have raised their norms may be increased in the near future'. Then came the crux of the whole argument:

> At the same time, the Politbureau considers it completely wrong to effect the 10% working norm increase in publicly owned enterprises by administrative measures. Working norms cannot and must not be raised by administrative methods, but solely by means of persuasion and voluntary decision.[55]

It was not the raising of the norms that was wrong, it was the way they were being raised. In effect, the Party had returned to the more informal position taken on the norms before the resolution of the 13th Session of the Central Committee on May 13-14. As the *Neues Deutschland* article of June 14 had further demonstrated, the spirit of the new Course called for persuasion rather than arbitrary administrative compulsion.

Whether the *Tribuene* article and the Politbureau pronouncement which followed it reflected confusion and conflict at the summit, or whether the latter declaration was the result of the pressure exerted by striking workers, it is safe to say that the one set off the demonstrations while the other failed to stop them. Bloc 40 on the Stalinallee remained the focal point. Here a member of the trade union committee read the *Tribuene* article to the workers, as an answer to their resolution of the previous day. The representative who had been summoned the previous day arrived at 8.30 a.m. to talk about the norms, but he was met with angry cries. It was decided to send the two delegates to Grotewohl or Ulbricht, despite the answer given in Lehmann's article. Suddenly a brigadier came forward with an improvised speech, and shouted that now was the time to act. Not only the delegates but everyone must go. One worker there present has recounted the emotional relief and great support evoked by this call to action:

> A fellow worker stepped forward: I place before you the choice: He who is with us, step to the right; he who is not

[54] *Ibid.* See also: Bundesministerium für Gesamtdeutsche Fragen, *op. cit.*, Doc. 26, pp. 45-6.   [55] *Ibid.*

with us, step to the left. The whole crowd now went to the right. I must say, that I stood with tears in my eyes. I saw that here not only empty words were being spoken, but words were being turned into action.[56]

Several painters and carpenters prepared a crude banner bearing the words: 'We demand a lowering of the norms.' Symbolically, on the other side there ran the slogan, now crossed out: 'On the Occasion of May 1 Bloc 40 Has Voluntarily Raised Its Norms by 10%.' Led by their new slogan, the workers streamed down the Stalinallee, while others went to the sites on the nearby Ruedersdorferstrasse to collect more workers.[57] Figures vary as to the number who marched from Bloc 40 in the beginning: some say 80, others say 300.[58] However, all reports agree that the march began around 9.00 a.m., and within an hour there were between 1,000 and 2,000 construction workers collected from the construction sites in the Stalinallee. Work had stopped everywhere, but not without difficulty in some places. For instance, the workers on site G—South had originally stood fast at their jobs, because trade union functionaries stood there to prevent anyone's leaving. The procession stopped at the site, while its members shouted to their fellow workers; a battle of words lasted about ten minutes. Then the workers broke loose, rushed past the functionaries and joined the procession.[59]

With movement down the Stalinallee toward Alexanderplatz at about 11.00, and from then to the centre of the city—across the Lustgarten (Marx and Engels Platz), down Unter den Linden to Wilhelmstrasse, all concentrating at the 'House of Ministries' (the main government building) at the corner of Wilhelmstrasse and Leipziger by approximately 2.00 in the afternoon, one finds the growth of a mass demonstration which was to grow into a full-fledged uprising by the next day. The multi-faceted growth of this revolutionary upsurge during June 16-17 throughout the whole zone has been the subject of a recent book, not to speak of the numerous articles dealing with particular aspects of the movement.[60] Rather than recapitulating in brief what has been given previously in such detail, the concluding paragraphs of this paper will touch upon certain

---

[56] Joachim G. Leithäuser (ed.), *op. cit.*, p. 14.   [57] *Id.*, pp. 13-14.
[58] The lower estimate is given in 'Chronik des Juni-Aufstandes', *S.B.Z. Archiv* (5 July 1953), p. 197; also International Confederation of Free Trade Unions, *op. cit.*, p. 10. The upper estimate is contained in Stefan Brant, *op. cit.*, p. 103.
[59] Joachim G. Leithäuser (ed.), *op. cit.*, p. 14.
[60] The book has recently been translated from the original German: Stefan Brant, *The East German Rising* (London, 1955).

characteristics of the rebellion and any significance it may have had for Communist policy in the zone.

III

In retrospect the East German riots appear as spontaneous outbursts among the working class which found sympathy in all sections of the population. Whatever importance one attributes to the mass support the rebellion received, it cannot be denied that the working class was and remained from the beginning the active nucleus of the movement. By June 16 the connections of the S.E.D. with this class had been so weakened that it took only the initial outbreak in Berlin to sever them. The sudden and blundering change of policy forced on the regime from without, and the attempt to implement the old norms policy already repudiated by the workers, were a combustible combination. The workers, already in a restive state from the harshness of the previous policy, took strength from the shattered morale of the Party following the about-face in policy. Its shattered self-confidence, and the obvious lack of confidence in its ability shown by the Soviet authorities, left the S.E.D. in no condition to force its demands on anyone, least of all the one cohesive class left in Eastern Germany.

Though the demonstrations and strikes began over the question of working norms, they soon went far beyond to more basic economic and political problems. The culmination was nothing less than a demand for the removal of the Government. Its penitence was not enough to placate the strikers and demonstrators. Somehow they felt that the Soviet Occupation Authority, already upset by the dire conditions brought about by past policy, would let the regime fall under the popular pressure. At the same time, there seemed no clear programme for unity with the regime in Western Germany. For instance, a crude banner displayed in Magdeburg on June 17 read: 'Clear up your mess in Bonn, for we are going to sweep our house clean in Eastern Germany.' Another doggerel scrawled out on walls and boards read: 'Out with Ulbricht and Adenauer. We want to deal with Ollenhauer.'[61] There was general agreement on what they did not want—the continued puppet S.E.D. government—and also on what they wanted—German unity and a better standard of living; however, this did not necessarily include a wholesale approval of the specific system established in Western Germany.

The cohesiveness of the working class was shown in a most

[61] Terence Prittie, *Manchester Guardian*, June 24, 1953.

dramatic way: the demonstrations and strikes were carried out in good order under the loose leadership of strike committees elected by acclamation at unorganized meetings. The local organization and co-ordination between neighbouring factories are all the more remarkable in view of the fact that the trade union in Eastern Germany has become another arm of the state. The strikes had to be directed without the benefits of any established channels of control. One writer has traced this natural discipline and organization to two factors: (1) a tradition of self-activity of the German workers, meaning the ability to act in an organized formal organization, or to act in accordance with political aims in the absence of formal political leadership; (2) cohesiveness and stability of the German working class, due to its previous slow growth and unity in face of opposition from the officer and capitalist elements throughout German history.[62] In any event it is important to remember that the working class in Eastern Germany, as in any Communist state, is the base upon which the regime rests itself in theory. Also, it was the one class untouched by expropriations and persecution following 1945. By state policy, the working class more than any other section of the population would have the ability to take unified action.

Control and organization were initially successful locally; there was no co-ordinated network throughout the zone. Although the radio broadcasts from Western Berlin telling of the mass demonstration on June 16 had sparked risings throughout the zone, these individual movements lacked contacts with each other or even knowledge of one another's successes. Once the Soviet troops acted, they were bound to collapse. They had shouted and pushed away unarmed the weak and hesitating German authority, but they had neither the will nor the facility to act against the unified opposition presented by the Soviet armed forces.

Although it is impossible to ascertain definitely how many were killed or wounded in the demonstrations, as well as the numbers executed or arrested thereafter, the various estimates available do indicate the magnitude of the disturbances. On June 25, Wilhelm Zaisser, the Minister of State Security (Staatsicherheit), gave to a meeting of the Council of Ministers these official figures for the whole zone: 25 dead, including 3 from the Volkspolizei, 1 from the State Security Service, 2 innocent civilian bystanders and 19 demonstrators; 378 wounded

---

[62] H. Brand, 'East Germany: The Uprising of June 17', *Dissent* (Winter 1954), p. 33.

including 191 from the Volkspolizei, 61 innocent civilian by-standers and 126 demonstrators. [63]

According to an unidentified source in a West Berlin newspaper, *Die Welt*, on July 15, Zaisser reported to Colonel Ilnitzki in the Secret Police of the Soviet High Commission that 569 had died on and after June 17 in both the zone and East Berlin, and 1,744 had been wounded. Of the dead, 267 were demonstrators killed at the time, 116 were Party functionaries and State Security members killed during the demonstrations, 141 were shot under martial law, 14 were hanged under death sentences passed by zonal courts, and 31 were shot during violations of the strict curfew. Of the 141 shot under martial law, 52 were reported to be members of the Volkspolizei or State Security Service who refused to obey orders. Of the 1,744 wounded, 1,071 were demonstrating, 645 were Party functionaries and State Security members, and 28 were hurt while violating the curfew. Zaisser's report also stated the Soviets had 18 dead and 126 wounded. Even more striking were the figures given about the numbers arrested up to July 10. The number of demonstrators arrested was put at 5,143, of which 2,917 were released without sentence, 1,076 were given jail sentences amounting in aggregate to 6,321 years, and 1,150 were still under investigation. Besides this, 1,756 Volkspolizei, members of the State Security Service and S.E.D. were arrested for not proceeding energetically enough against the demonstrators. Although all these figures cannot be checked, their very detail —together with the wide number of reports given by refugees during the days after the riots—tempts one to believe that they are at least far more representative than the official figures initially released. [64]

It is hard to discern any permanent influence of the riots on overall Communist policy in Germany. Certainly in the short run they hurried the introduction of new reforms and gained for the working class the benefits they had been denied in the first announcements. They showed the real weakness of the S.E.D. and how litle foundation the regime had in the people. The frank admissions of the Party both before and after the riots give official substantiation to what the riots had shown most dramatically. However, they did not topple the regime. Rather, such mass disapprobation showed the Russians that if

[63] British Broadcasting Corporation, *op. cit.*, No. 215, p. 35. Wilhelm Cornides and Helmut Löschorn, 'Materialen zu den Ereignissen des 16 und 17 Juni 1953 in Berlin und der S.B.Z.', *op. cit.*, p. 5834.

[64] Wilhelm Cornides und Helmut Löschorn, 'Materialen zu den Ereignissen des 16 und 17 Juni 1953 in Berlin und der S.B.Z.', *op. cit.*, pp. 5834-5.

they wanted to constitute the Eastern German government as a viable instrument of authority to deal with the Western German authorities about unification, much must be done to regain it some modicum of support among its own subjects. It was reform of the regime's policy, not the abandonment of the regime, which the Soviets chose.

NEW TRENDS IN SOVIET POLICY TOWARDS ISLAM

By Geoffrey Wheeler

AMONG the many eastern problems now exercising the mind of the Soviet Ministry of Foreign Affairs must be that of how best to reconcile the classic Marxist attitude of uncompromising hostility towards Islam with the new policy of rapprochement with independent Muslim countries.

Although Islam falls within the general category of 'beliefs in the supernatural' to which Marxist philosophy takes such strong exception, it has always been regarded as potentially more obnoxious than any other creed practised in the U.S.S.R. This is partly because it has a universal character and influence not possessed by the predominant religion, the Orthodox Church of Russia, and partly because it has never, like Christianity, undergone a reformation or renaissance which could loosen the bonds of mediaevalism and bring both dogma and practice into line with modern life. The Soviet authorities have constantly been assailed by or have simulated a fear, which at times appears unreasonable and exaggerated, of the 'cosmopolitan' influence of Islam among its adherents in the U.S.S.R. They are also convinced that the Muslim way of life is incompatible with modern materialism and 'progress'.

Dissatisfaction with the social and judicial principles of Islam has of course been apparent among the intelligentsia in Muslim countries for many years and has found expression in attitudes ranging from passive scepticism to active secularism. Actual hostility to the essentials of Islam has so far, however, been confined to the relatively sparse ranks of the Communists and their supporters. Middle Eastern governments have occasionally enacted legislation prohibiting such old-established traditional practices as public flagellation, the veiling of women and the wearing of certain traditional types of head-dress. In Turkey religious instruction was for a time excluded from the curricula of state schools and the use of Arabic as the liturgical language partly forbidden. Such measures have always been defended on utilitarian and nationalist grounds and as such have gained a considerable measure of support. But no government of an independent Muslim country, however sceptical it might be at heart, has so far engaged in or permitted any campaign of obloquy or ridicule directed against essential Islamic dogma and practice. The Soviet government, on the other hand, while it has refrained from legislation against religious and traditional observance, has never concealed its disapprobation of Islamic practice and its contempt for Muslim beliefs. Apart from a few brief respites necessitated by such circumstances as the collective Muslim opposition to the Soviet regime after the Civil War, and World War II, the authorities have until quite recently maintained a steady stream of derisive anti-Islamic propaganda.

As yet little is known of the methods which the Soviet government intend to use to gain the goodwill of the independent Muslim world. They will no doubt give prominence to political and economic gestures; but it seems unlikely that they will ignore the need for extending their cultural influence. In any event they may be expected to draw on their political, economic and cultural experiences with the 20,000,000 Muslim inhabitants of the U.S.S.R. They will also give serious thought to the effect which their attitude towards their new-found Muslim friends abroad may have on their own Muslims, whose continued attachment to feudal and religious survivals they constantly deprecate.

During the past three years some important work on the position of the Muslims of the U.S.S.R. has appeared in French and English. This includes *Essai sur L'Islam en U.R.S.S.* by V. Monteil, 'Les Peuples Musulmans de L'U.R.S.S. et les Soviets', an article in four parts by A. Bennigsen published in *L'Afrique et L'Asie* in 1953, and finally two articles by Dr Richard Pipes on the Muslims of Soviet Central Asia published in *Middle East Journal* in 1955. Between them these writers have collected most of the available data, the first two largely from Soviet publications and the last from interrogations of refugees, and they are all agreed that the Soviet government has made and was, at any rate until 1954, still making intensive efforts to extirpate Islamic culture from the life of the indigenous Muslim population. On the degree of success so far achieved they are less unanimous, Dr Pipes being less pessimistic about the survival of Islam than the two French writers.

All this work is of great interest and importance, but there are other lines of enquiry which are equally important and necessary if the potentialities of the future Soviet policy towards the Muslim East are to be thoroughly understood. The first is the history of the Russian Muslims' relations with the government of Russia both before and after the Revolution. Secondly, the current political, economic and cultural developments in the six nominally Muslim Soviet Socialist Republics and numerous Autonomous S.S.R.s of the Soviet Union; and thirdly the examination of Soviet publications on eastern subjects, the volume and significance of which are now considerable.

Soviet historians have been at great pains to trace the growth of national sentiment and desire for national self-expression among the many Muslim peoples who came under Russian domination at various times from the sixteenth century onwards. Their task is a difficult one: they have to show the Muslims as constantly loving and looking up to the Russian people, as hating their feudal and imperialist taskmasters, and as resenting the influence of clericalism and the Arab and Persian culture which followed in its train. Even Western writers speak of the rise of 'nationalism' among Muslim minorities, but in fact, it may be doubted whether nationalism is an appropriate description of the different stirrings and expressions of discontent which took place among the Muslim peoples of Russia during the nineteenth Century, or of those which developed after the Revolution. There were four kinds of movement: liberal reformist movements like those of Gasprinskiy among the Tartars; clerical or religious movements which sometimes resorted to violence; international movements vaguely connected with pan-Islam and pan-Turanianism; and finally a few instances of something approaching nationalist movements in the accepted sense in the Volga and Ural regions, Transcaucasia and Kazakhstan. Only in Bashkiria and Kazakhstan, however, were there clear manifestations of that most characteristic feature of nationalism—a desire to exclude foreign, that is, Russian and Ukrainian, settlers. Only the liberal intelligentsia was capable of grasping the political implications of pan-Turanianism and pan-Islam, and after the Revolution they received no material support from Turkey or much spiritual inspiration from the Islamic world outside the U.S.S.R. In any event, neither pan-Turanianism nor pan-Islam can properly be described as nationalism. Islam in particular is fundamentally opposed to nationalism the rise of which has seriously undermined its influence.

The first reaction which the Revolution had on the Muslims of Russia was to suggest to their intelligentsia the possibility of 'a revolution in the East' implemented by a Muslim federation begun in Russia and gradually extending to adjacent Muslim countries. Although this possibility appears at one time to have held some attraction for Stalin, it was on the whole regarded with disfavour by the central Soviet authorities. There are, indeed, strong grounds for believing that the precise labelling of the various peoples as Uzbeks, Kazakhs, Turkmens and so on, and the allotment to them of territories bearing their name, was the result not so much of pressure by the peoples themselves for individual recognition as of the conviction in the minds of the central authorities that the creation of a number of nominally independent 'national' republics was the best way of countering the potential threat of united Muslim opposition.

Whether the adoption of 'nationalism' as an antidote to Islam was the result of shrewd calculation, or merely an example of the 'beginner's luck' which so often attends revolutions, is a matter for speculation. Events certainly played into the hands of the Soviet authorities, for their plans coincided not only with the collapse of the Ottoman empire consequent on Turkey's defeat in 1918, but with the abolition of the caliphate which occurred a few years later. These blows to the temporal and spiritual prestige of Islam greatly facilitated the Soviet task: with the supranational influence of Islam on the wane the imposition of synthetic nationalism on the unsophisticated Muslim peoples of Russia became relatively easy.

The self-assurance with which the Soviet government is now courting the independent countries of the Middle East and South Asia may be partly justified by circumstances; or it may be assumed for propaganda purposes; or finally, it may spring from an imperfect appreciation of the situation and a mistaken if sincere belief in the attractions which the communist conception of nationalism would hold for the Muslim peoples outside the Soviet Union. The Soviet government may well believe that the same spectacular material progress which it has achieved among the Muslim peoples held in thrall by the Tsarist military conquests of the eighteenth and nineteenth centuries can be extended to countries and peoples but lately released from the relatively easy yoke of the Ottoman Empire. Among their often apt stigmatizations of independent Eastern governments as reactionary and predatory Soviet propagandists include the charge that these governments are 'the lackeys of Western imperialism', and the Soviet government evidently believes quite genuinely that the toiling masses of the East would greatly prefer to be under Soviet tutelage, if not actually merged in the Soviet Union. This resembles the 'diehard imperialist' attitude which is fast being abandoned in the West, though whether from weakness or enlightenment is not always certain. How the Soviet government would react to expressions of unwillingness to accept their economic and political mentorship, which might eventually succeed the early protestations of delight at the new Soviet overtures, remains to be seen.

Reference has already been made to the likelihood of the Soviet government drawing on the experience it has gained in raising the productivity of Muslim peoples inside the U.S.S.R. The means employed there have included the extensive development of general and technical education, the sovietization and russianization of traditional cultures, the mechanization and collectivization of agriculture, and the introduction of skilled and unskilled labour from the European parts of the Union. Since it is to be expected that at least some of the same methods will be attempted in independent countries it is important to examine the degree of success which has so far attended them in areas such as Central Asia and Kazakhstan. Contrary to widespread belief it is possible to construct a coherent and accurate picture of current economic and cultural developments in these areas by a cumulative study of Soviet publications. With a few exceptions these publications range over almost every kind of human activity and reflect not only the progress being achieved but also the grave problems characteristic of undeveloped areas and traditional cultures which are still being encountered. Research work on these subjects is being conducted in the West but not all of it is informed by the necessary objectivity. There has long been a tendency to 'play down' Soviet material achievements in the eastern parts of the Union, to exaggerate local opposition and even to suggest that Soviet economy in these regions is on the brink of collapse. Realization that the situation in Soviet Asia is not so bad as the West would have them believe, and may in some respects be better than in their own countries, has contributed powerfully to the temporary swing of Middle Eastern opinion in favour of the U.S.S.R. On the other hand, far too little has been made known about the regimentation of traditional culture, particularly in the matter of the russianization of local languages.

Perhaps the greatest lacuna is to be found in the matter of examining Soviet publications on affairs and problems pertaining to the Islamic world in general, including independent Muslim countries. Although the volume of these publications has greatly increased of late they have been steadily appearing for the past thirty years. As early as 1924 the Leningrad Oriental

Institute (since merged in the Moscow Academy of Sciences) began to produce works which, although for the most part written by orientalists of the previous regime, bore evidence of a new approach. The claims of classical antiquity were not to be disregarded, but the main emphasis was to be on modern social and political developments and on the modern as opposed to the classical forms of eastern languages.

Until recently Soviet attention has been focussed principally on the Muslim peoples living in the U.S.S.R., but even before the war some important works were produced on Middle Eastern and South Asian languages and history. Although an idea of the quantity and range of Soviet publications on Islamic subjects can readily be obtained from bibliographies and book catalogues, their contents and importance are matters which have so far received scant attention in the West. This is partly due to the fact that the Russian language is not ordinarily included in the linguistic equipment of Western orientalists, and partly because almost all Soviet oriental research is known to be informed by Marxist political considerations. The difference between the Western and Soviet approaches to Islamic studies is indeed very marked. Most Western scholars embarking on the study of Islamic history, religion, philosophy and ethics, do so in a spirit of sympathy and respect. Soviet scholars, on the other hand, while admitting the importance of Islam, are largely concerned with the process of *razoblacheniye*, that is, with the unmasking of what they regard as the deadening effect of an outworn way of life. The strictly 'scientific' approach on which Marxism insists brings to Islamic studies the same kind of enthusiasm which a bacteriologist brings to the study of the cause, course, consequences, and ultimately to the eradication, of a pernicious disease.

Soviet academic authorities have for their part always been aware and highly critical of the Western attitude towards Islamic studies. They now, however, advocate much closer attention to the work of Russian and foreign 'bourgeois' orientalists, which they consider contains much that is of value for Soviet scholars. There is so far little sign of a similar realization on the part of Western scholarship. In linguistics and philology Soviet scholarship has produced much valuable work, particularly that dealing with the modern forms of such languages as Arabic and Persian, of which little or no cognizance or advantage has been taken by the West. Again, comparatively little notice has yet been taken by the West of the vast work of elaboration and russification of the Turkic languages of Central

Asia and the Caucasus carried out by Soviet orientalists. This work may be repugnant to Western scholars, but it is of great importance and bears evidence of considerable learning and research. The same can be said of much Soviet writing on eastern history and culture. Its accuracy, objectivity and the positive contribution which it makes to learning may be doubted; but its examination is essential if the nature and potentialities of Soviet eastern policies are to be properly apprehended.

An article published in *Kommunist* of May 1955 makes it clear that the authorities are by no means satisfied with what has so far been achieved. A great expansion of oriental studies is envisaged and already the volume of published work on the history, ethnography, literature, economics and politics of the independent Muslim East has greatly increased. During 1955 six issues appeared of a new periodical entitled *Sovetskoye Vostokovedeniye* (Soviet Oriental Studies) which is evidently intended to carry the bulk of the new material and can be expected to reflect the trend of modern Soviet policy at least in cultural matters.

The study of the Soviet attitude towards Islam has been dangerously neglected in the past and this will make it all the more difficult to understand the future development of Soviet policy. It need not be supposed that the Soviet task will be an easy one. The newest arrival on the Middle Eastern stage can usually be sure of engaging the interest of his audience especially if his patter includes colourful abuse of previous performers; but to sustain that interest requires patience and understanding. The scathing Soviet condemnation of everything done by the Western powers need not perhaps be taken too seriously, but the Soviet government has certainly much to learn from the West's mistakes as well as from its own ill-starred attempts to subvert countries like Persia. It cannot fail to be aware that closer relations with the independent Muslim East may react on Central Asia and the Caucasus, and the decree of November 11, 1954, on 'certain mistakes in the conduct of scientific and atheistic propaganda' has already had what was presumably the intended effect of virtually putting a stop to the more offensive type of anti-Islamic propaganda. This seems a normal and reasonable precaution; but Soviet policy may contain many novelties. In the light of their own failures and successes both in the past and in the future they will have to decide such questions as whether to play off nationalism against Islam as they did in the early days of the Revolution, whether to ignore Islam or exploit it, whether something might not even be gained by staging an Islamic renaissance under Soviet auspices. Careful study of the past and present history of Russia's dealings with Islam and of current Soviet writing on the subject will at least minimize the chances of disagreeable surprise.

IN A SOVIET ISOLATOR

By W. Claudius

IN autumn 1950 I was arrested in Berlin by the Soviet State
Security and charged with alleged espionage. On the next
stages of my 'via crucis' I did not expect to discover anything
new, considering the fact that during World War II I happened
to be, for two years, a prisoner of the Gestapo. It was a mistake.
The criminal brutality of the Gestapo was certainly inhuman.
But their brutality was an individual one. Everything depended
on the person who was interrogating you. If he was a convinced
Nazi, plus a sadist, then in his rage and hate he was able even
to kill you. But if you were lucky enough to be interrogated by
an old policeman, serving already the third regime—then
during the whole inquiry, you were not even touched.

In the case of the M.G.B. (Cheka) (M.G.B.—Ministry of
State Security) the brutality is collective and based almost on
scientific research. Interrogators are trained in every step of
brutality, but employ it only on special orders. Personally the
M.G.B. interrogator could be a nice chap—far from being a
sadist, or even hating his prisoner-victim. On Sunday afternoon,
when he is Officer in Charge, he may invite the prisoner to share
with him a couple of sandwiches and a bottle of beer, and be
sincerely friendly to him. The next day, on orders, he may
shout at him, maltreat and punish him, getting excited in an
artificial way and sometimes even laughing about it.

From the Headquarters of the Staatsicherheitsdienst (East
German State Security, 'Stasi' as it is called in Germany) in
Eastern Berlin, where I was kept for a few days, I was brought
to the M.G.B. Headquarters in Germany at Karlshorst—
Berlin. To make a true picture it must be said that a prisoner
once transferred from the 'Stasi' to the M.G.B. prison, felt, in
a certain sense, much easier. It was obviously due to the difference between the individual brutality of the German Communists, 'Volkspolizei' N.C.O.s, and the collective brutality of
their Russian colleagues—M.G.B. N.C.O.s, acting on special
orders only.

Actually I was brought to Karlshorst M.G.B. Headquarters
in the afternoon. At 11 o'clock at night I was glad to have a rest.

About half an hour after I lay down I was brought to my interrogator for my first interrogation at M.G.B. Headquarters. Major (later Lieutenant-Colonel) M. seemed to be very pleased to see me. At first he joked and spoke about innocent things, offered me a cigarette, and then, suddenly, in the old Cheka manner, asked me not to sabotage the enquiry but to hand over at once all my agents in Eastern Germany and other 'peoples democracies'. As I had never had any agents in Eastern Germany or any other country, I naturally could not satisfy the kind request of the 'Citizen Major'.

In the following month I was taught, by several means of physical torture and psychological tricks, to confess my 'criminal activities'—which I naturally, at the first possible moment, withdrew. In this way, being considered a specially dangerous subject and a still-resisting enemy, I was brought to the M.G.B. Headquarters in Moscow, the notorious Lubyanka. There I was subjected to further interrogation—no change of methods, just of persons. Finally in May 1952 at the transit prison ('Presylka') of Krasnaia Presna in Moscow, I was presented with an administrative decision of the Special Commission of the Ministry of State Security (O.S.O.) according to which I was sentenced 'for espionage and counter-revolutionary activities' to ten years' prison isolation.

The political isolators in Soviet Russia serve four main purposes. First, to hide a V.I.P. prisoner from the whole world. Second to punish a considered potential enemy with isolation and slow starvation. Thirdly to isolate potential enemies—mostly intellectuals—from the mass of the other prisoners kept in forced labour camps; and fourthly to prevent dangerous subjects from having any freedom of movement in forced labour camps.

In very specific cases the isolator can be considered as the purgatory on the way to freedom. This was, for instance, the case of approximately 1,500 Austrians, who at the end of 1952 were transferred from forced labour camps to isolators, and then finally in June 1955 liberated.

In conversations with cell-mates, I found out that there are in Soviet Russia—in spite of thousands of forced labour camps—only a few isolators. We knew five of them: 1. Vladimir; 2. Novocherkask; 3. Ufa; 4. Verkhne-Uralsk; and 5. Aleksandrovsk. This numeration is done in this way officially in Russia, and runs geographically from west to east and No. 5 is Aleksandrovsk in East Siberia. I do not think there are many more of these isolators apart from some which are absolutely secret and perhaps used for special purposes.

The regime and food in all these isolators (I can vouch for four of them) was almost the same. There was a certain deviation in general conditions due to the particular severity of the warden and his staff and also in view of different climatic conditions. Anyhow, based on the experiences of former cell-mates and on my own, I can state that the Aleksandrovsk isolator must be considered as the worst of these institutions. All five isolators were administered till March 1953 by the M.G.B.; for instance Verkhne-Uralsk was officially called M.G.B. prison No. 4.

After the fusion of the M.G.B. with the M.V.D. (Ministry of Interior) the isolators became M.V.D. prisons—without any change of personnel. After the creation of the Committee of State Security (K.G.B.) in March-April 1954 the isolators remained under the control of the M.V.D., but the so-called Operative Officer (in fact, the Commissar) was directly attached to this new institution.

The first political isolator I was brought to in May 1952, was Verkhne-Uralsk (No. 4) forty miles from Magnitogorsk. Verkhne-Uralsk itself is a small town (I would say a large village) of 10,000 inhabitants, and it is the centre of the same named district in the Chelyabinsk area.

The prison which served as this isolator was built during World War I, by German and Austrian P.O.W.s. It was a three-floor building in red stone, with some wooden huts and several small exercise yards—all surrounded by a high wooden fence. In every corner of the fenced yard there was a watch-tower, with spotlight. There M.G.B. soldiers were exchanged every two hours, during the whole twenty-four.

Entering this isolator for the first time you thought yourself in a church. In spite of large corridors, absolute silence reigned in the building. This was due to the prohibition of prisoners speaking loudly in their cells. On every floor, there were six long common cells (for ten to twenty-five people) and four small cells (for three to eight people). In the cellar outside the kitchen were situated the punishment cells and also three big common cells. The solitary confinement cells were on an interior floor. This interior floor had been built up into the building within the last few years and had altogether twenty-one small cells, for one or two people. On every floor there were two lavatories (without proper drainage)which could be used only in the early morning and in the late evening. There, one could wash—even in winter—provided the pipes were not frozen. Average winter temperatures were minus 20° centigrade.

Women prisoners were kept in the corner of the third floor, where the former prison chapel had once been situated and which was now transformed into a surgery. The regime in the isolator was very rigid. At six o'clock in the morning, reveille, and at seven o'clock 1lb. of something in English called bread —indeed it was a black mass cooked, with a content of something like 60% water. Then 1 oz. or less of sugar and boiled water containing some ersatz coffee, and 3 oz of herring, generally of very bad quality.

Between eight and one o'clock you were led into the fenced exercise yard—approximately twenty-five feet by twenty-five, where you were watched every minute by a special yard warder, so that you could not communicate with the neighbouring yard and in this way break the segregation rules. Between one and two o'clock lunch was distributed. Mostly a fatless cabbage soup and 'Kasha'. After lunch you were allowed to rest for an hour. For dinner, between six and seven p.m. you received again a fatless soup with a few potatoes. At ten o'clock was the retreat. Due to this very small ration several of us died, and almost everybody, after a certain time, became distrophic. Medical treatment was very bad. The isolator doctor was almost always drunk and the whole responsibility was left to three young Komsomol nurses, who failed to take the necessary steps in cases of serious illness because of their ignorance. Also, being instructed every week in the isolator Komsomol cell about vigilance against enemies (as we were considered), they were not very interested in helping us.

There was, however, one way to get supplementary food and medical treatment. This was to become a traitor to one's cell-mates and a spy for one's enemies. The so-called Operative Officer of the isolator (the Commissar) tried to get as much information as possible about what was going on in the common cells. What people said. What they were planning and thinking. Outside of this purely internal material, he was very eager to report to Moscow any names of accomplices—or would-be accomplices—still in freedom. In this way the Commissar set up a whole net-work of stool-pigeons including the cells of solitary confinement. His agents he found almost always among Soviet citizens, because for them it seemed a true chance (as they thought, and perhaps rightly) to get free. And then, a Soviet citizen who 'played' the man faithful to the Soviet regime, could hardly refuse such a 'patriotic proposal'. Naturally there were also some traitors—among foreigners—especially during the starvation period of 1950-53. All foreigners who accepted this very low and dishonest task were of limited intellectual calibre and of an inferior character. A clever foreigner knew that once liberated from Russia he would be checked and counter-checked, and finally anything could happen to him as a traitor. . . . Therefore traitors among the foreigners could be much more easily unmasked. And then they ceased to be of any value or use.

An underfed man could obtain from the doctor an invalid's supplementary food, only by the approval of the Commissar. Sometimes, mainly to camouflage his spy in a certain cell, even a decent man got the Commissar's approval.

In Verkhne-Uralsk there was a library of some 2,500 books, among them about 200 foreign books in English, German and French. The Library was a selection of Soviet political and economic literature, and Russian and Soviet fiction. In Aleksandrovsk we had a library of some 4,000 volumes. Among them very old books (for instance, a history of Russia, printed at the end of the eighteenth century) and many books published immediately after the Revolution—to-day on the Index. In Vladimir there were about 20,000 books, among them a few thousand foreign books. The prisoners could not use the library directly. The Librarian was a woman M.G.B.-N.C.O., below average intellect, who brought, every fortnight, to a solitary prisoner two books, and to each in a common cell one book.

Until Beria's arrest we occasionally got newspapers, local or central. But from October 1953 we regularly received the local daily paper and the Moscow *Pravda*. Soviet citizens in possession of money had to pay. From January 1954, we could subscribe to newspapers from satellite countries, and I, for instance, up to the time of my liberation took in almost daily the Eastern German paper *Neues Deutschland*.

Until Beria's arrest we did not regularly receive any cigarettes. From September 1953, we got ten Russian cigarettes daily: they were of bad quality, but at any rate they were cigarettes. Until 1953 we were not allowed to have any paper, pencils or pen, but after March 1953, we received monthly a copy-book and pencils.

The conditions of hygiene in Verkhne-Uralsk were not of the worst in summer: we could wash in the lavatory and every ten days we had a hot bath, which in practice meant hot water at our disposal. Before the bath we were shaved (with hair-cutting machines) and every four weeks we had a hair-cut—a bald head. After the bath we got clean underwear, Russian stockings ('partyanki') and a bed-sheet. No handkerchiefs or normal stockings were given to us. Soviet prisoners who had money could buy them in the canteen. The canteen was operated by an N.C.O., who came three times a month to deliver provisions. Every month one could buy 150 roubles worth of goods. The goods in the canteen were very expensive and of bad quality. The chief luxuries were bread, margarine and sugar.

Until December 1953 we had to wear striped prison garb—a pyjama-like jacket and trousers, and a fur coat, a Russian bushlat. After the autumn of 1953 we were allowed to wear our own clothes, so far as they were still in a wearable condition.

Most of the Soviet citizens could write to their next of kin. Until September 1953 they were allowed to write twice a year, and to receive 150 roubles a month. No visits or parcels were allowed. After September 1953 they could write monthly, and receive four parcels, each one of eight pounds in weight. No foreigners were allowed to write until September 1953. In the autumn of 1953 all foreigners sentenced by military court (mostly former German, Austrian and Japanese P.O.W.s, and some condemned war criminals) could write every month one Red Cross card and receive four parcels a month. As from March 1955 all foreigners—even those sentenced in an administrative way by O.S.O.—could enjoy these privileges.

No work was allowed to be carried out by political prisoners. The internal work inside the isolator was done by free hired people, and outside the prison by common criminals, whom we never saw. Several among us applied to Moscow for permission to get any sort of work, but this was categorically refused. Inasmuch as one could not work one had to find a way of employing one's time rationally, to prevent mental disease. Reading was limited to the number of books we got every fortnight; sleeping during the day was not allowed and, if one was caught, one was punished by carcer—punishment cells. In the common cells people were in a much better position: they could talk to each other. But after two or three months (being together twenty-four hours of each day) one knew almost every step in the life of one's interlocutor. We could also play dominoes or chess, but generally quarrels would start about the game, and it soon had to be abandoned. So rational people tried to learn something, and to teach others. Until 1953 this was almost dangerous, as the stool-pigeons of the cells (and every cell had to have one) reported to the Commissar, and you were summoned and questioned: 'Why, for instance, do you study Russian? To work as a spy afterwards, against the U.S.S.R.?' One had to be very careful in answering, because the least that could happen was to be transferred into a solitary cell.

After autumn 1953 these things changed, and it even happened that people asked to be transferred, to have an opportunity of learning this or that subject.

In the solitary cells, after six months most people started to have visions, and talked to themselves. To avoid going mad, one had to submit oneself to a very rigid regime of definite intellectual activity, as, for instance, dealing every day with a different historical subject, translating from books or newspapers into other languages, and resolving mathematical problems. The general conditions and the treatment changed abruptly after the death of Stalin:

(1) Now we could rest whenever we wanted during the day;
(2) We were no longer humiliated by having to wear striped prison garb;
(3) Most people got permission to write, and to receive parcels;
(4) People kept in solitary confinement (for instance, myself) were transferred into common cells;
(5) We now got cigarettes, newspapers and writing materials;
(6) Food increase: we got more bread, more potatoes and cereals, and even some hash with the soup;
(7) We were not punished for every minor transgression; and
(8) The arbitrary actions of the whole staff towards the prisoners were limited by the right of the prisoners themselves to apply now three times monthly to higher Soviet authorities in sealed letters.

There were two other points which burdened the prisoners' minds very heavily. The first was anxiety about one's relatives, thousands of miles away, without any news. The best thing was not to think about it at all, but there were days, as for instance at Christmas, when you had to think. The second was the sexual problem. Until 1953, when people were down and out and under-fed, this question was not a problem for us. Everybody was dreaming only about a good meal. But, for female prisoners, this problem was always a central one, and even during the biggest starvation period never ceased to be acute. We could often hear from the women's cells the rages of hysteria which were almost always quelled by the isolator administration with carcer. The young women suffered more from this acute problem than from hunger or from segregation.

After the majority among us started to receive parcels and to recover in part physically (due to a wonderful international solidarity and comradeship, the matter covered even those without parcels) this problem started to make itself felt, and one had to control oneself, to withstand certain seductions of an unnatural character.

Then things started to change outside, and in our small world also. Everybody—Soviet citizens and foreigners—began to hope that freedom might be not so far away. In August 1953 about a hundred foreigners (mostly Austrians) were suddenly released; then, in December, forty women prisoners were also released. Now everyone was convinced that our turn would soon come too. It came very soon. Indeed, in March 1954 our whole prison was to be transferred. Approximately 180 of them (among them myself) went east—3,500 miles from Moscow—to Isolator No. 5 (Aleksandrovsky Central). About 150 (mostly sick and old people) were transferred to Isolator No. 1, Vladimir.

The general disappointment while moving to the east (towards Irkutsk) instead of west—towards Moscow and Europe—changed almost to desperation when we arrived at Aleksandrovsky. Aleksandrovsky is a small village (about 500 inhabitants, mostly connected directly or indirectly with the isolator) in East Siberia, near Lake Baikal, fifty miles from Irkutsk. The isolator is actually the old Dekabrist Prison, built under Nicholas I after 1825. The general conditions, including the regime and hygiene, were much worse than in Verkhne-Uralsk. The prison was a big, shabby, two-storeyed building, with a damaged ceiling and a completely damp atmosphere. After only three months one developed rheumatic pains. The cultural level of the warders was much inferior to the warders of Verkhne Uralsk, and their way of swearing while talking to you was particularly offensive. On the other hand, these primitive guards, once they were attached to you, respecting you because of your patience, intelligence and even generosity (in view of our parcels from the western world), would talk to you on any topic, but only when alone with us. Sometimes they told us very interesting things. In Verkhne-Uralsk this would not have been possible. There the warders were forbidden to talk to us at all. As a matter of fact, in Verkhne-Uralsk I once asked a woman warder a question. She slammed down the food hatch angrily and when I protested against her vehemence she said she was paid not to talk to me.

At the end of 1954 the regime became milder and at Christmas 1954, because of the large quantities of parcels (about 500 for some 200 foreigners) we were, for the first time, celebrating

Christmas in Russia with almost everything (apart from spirits) we could desire.

Generally the prisoners in the isolators could be divided into the following main groups and categories.

I. *Soviet citizens (within the 1938 frontiers):*
  (1) Old Communist Party Guard (Trotskyist and Buk-harinist).
  (2) Other old Revolutionaries (Mensheviks, S.R.s, etc.).
  (3) Old Orthodox priests and nuns.
  (4) Anti-Stalin-Party-Opposition, among the young Soviet generation (Rabochaya Oppositsiya), arrested mainly after 1947.
  (5) Soviet intellectuals and army officers—'Boltuni'—(under para. 58-10)—arrested between 1947 and 1952 for alleged anti-Soviet propaganda.
  (6) Soviet army officers, arrested and charged with 'indirect terrorism' and contact with the West (under paras. 58-8-17 and 58-1), friends and comrades of Zhukov, arrested after 1947.
  (7) Jewish intellectuals, would-be Zionists or nationalists, arrested between 1947 and 1953.
  (8) Russian and Ukrainian peasants, Baptists, Witnesses of Jehovah and other sectarians, arrested since 1945.
  (9) Former P.O.W.s in Germany (but not fighting against the Russians)—arrested for anti-Soviet propaganda; and
  (10) Former high-ranking Vlasov, S.S. and police officers and officials, mostly P.O.W.s in Germany, charged with high treason.

II. *Soviet Citizens—from countries occupied after 1938:*
  (1) Bourgeois intellectuals (Polish, West Ukrainian and Baltic) arrested after 1946 for alleged anti-Soviet propaganda.
  (2) Roman Catholic, Greek-Catholic, and Protestant clergy.
  (3) Leaders of Partisan groups against the Communists in the Baltic.

III. *Foreigners:*
  (1) Allied officers, including Ch'iang Kai-shek officers, kidnapped in Germany, Austria and Korea (Manchuria) after 1945 and mostly charged with espionage.
  (2) Western intellectuals (including anti-Nazis or non-Nazis from Germany and Austria) kidnapped after 1945 in Germany or Austria, for alleged espionage—some really

involved as resident agents of Western Intelligence Services.

(3) Family relatives of former Axis leaders ('Sippenhaft').

(4) High-ranking German (Austrian) and Japanese combatant army officers—former P.O.W.s—charged with alleged war crimes.

(5) Former high-ranking German and Japanese intelligence officers—former P.O.W.s—arrested after 1945 for espionage.

(6) Former high-ranking German, Japanese, and some Italian diplomats, seized since 1941 in different countries and charged with espionage.

(7) Former high-ranking Party officials of the 'N.S.D.A.P.', Gestapo, S.D. and German police, arrested after 1945 for war crimes.

(8) High-ranking politicians—anti-Communists or anti-Stalinists—from the satellite countries, mostly in power till 1947 and then arrested for treason and espionage.

(9) Austrians—brought to the isolators up to 1952 from forced labour camps—middle grade officials and officers charged with war crimes, would-be spies, and mostly arrested, or seized, in Austria between 1945 and 1952.

(10) Russian emigrés—citizens of foreign countries—taken in Germany, Austria or satellite countries after 1945, and charged with alleged high treason; and emigrés who voluntarily returned after 1945, and were arrested for anti-Soviet propaganda.

After the arrest of Beria, almost all Soviet citizens wrote to Malenkov (later to Bulganin), Khrushchev and the Prosecutor-General Rudenko, claiming their effective innocence and asking for their cases to be reviewed. All received answers direct from the Military Prosecutor, informing them that their cases were going to be reviewed and that they would be informed of the results. (In former times the answer would have been just one: 'The prisoner is guilty, and rightly sentenced.') The majority of the Soviet citizens, of both major groups, are still in prison waiting for those results. Anyhow, a small party of them (Group I, (5), (6) and (9)—alleged anti-Soviet propaganda) were lucky enough to be released (mostly in 1954) without any further discrimination, and some of them returned to their jobs in Moscow and Leningrad.

On the basis of the October Amnesty for collaboration with the Nazis, a certain number of this category were released before

I left. The majority of foreigners also applied to the highest Soviet authorities, some asking for their cases to be reviewed and others asking for an individual pardon to be granted to them by the Presidium of the Supreme Soviet. They also were notified by the Military Prosecutor that their cases would be reviewed and that they would be informed of the final result. No individual liberation occurred on the basis of a foreign prisoner's petition, but the majority of foreign prisoners were liberated and sent to their respective countries by the collective amnesty of the Presidium of the Supreme Soviet.

The first to depart were the Austrians, in May-June 1955; then, in September-October, prisoners belonging to the N.A.T.O. countries; and finally, in October, the repatriation of the Germans began. In October 1955 there still remained in the isolator of Aleksandrovsk the Japanese, the Nationalist Chinese, citizens of satellite countries, and some citizens of neutral countries.

Among the Soviet citizens whom I met personally in the isolator of Verkhne-Uralsk and in Aleksandrovsk were some of prominence who should be mentioned particularly. They were representatives of the Bolshevik Old Guard, as, for instance, *V. V. Astrov*, aged 62, the former Editor-in-Chief of *Pravda*; *N. A. Palatnikov*, aged 64, former Private Secretary to Trotsky; *V. D. Vershblovsky*, aged 60, former Editor-in-Chief of *Trud* (the trade union daily newspaper) and an active collaborator of Trotsky; *B. M. Kunitski*, aged 64, former Warden of the 'I.K.P.' (Institute of Red Professorship), a personal friend of Bukharin, and teacher of Malenkov and Pospelov, when they were sent as youngsters by the Komsomol to the I.K.P.

Among them the biography of *V. V. Astrov* is the most interesting to illustrate the end of the old Bolshevik Guard. Astrov, the son of a former Orthodox clergyman, was already, at the age of sixteen, a member of the old Social Democratic Party, and a steady follower of Lenin's Bolshevik line. During the October Revolution he was in charge of a Red Worker Guard Unit in Petersburg. During the Civil War he was a Commissar, first of a division and later of an army corps. After being wounded in 1919, he became Editor-in-Chief of the Smolensk *Pravda*. From 1920-24 he was one of the first pupils at the I.K.P. When the ideological monthly of the Party, *Bolshevik*, was founded Astrov, together with his close friend and leader, Bukharin, were among the founders. When Bukharin became Editor-in-Chief of the Central *Pravda*, Astrov joined the Editorial Board of the newspaper, and later became Editor-in-

Chief of the Leningrad *Pravda*. Towards the end of his career he became the Editor-in-Chief of the Central *Pravda*.

When he, together with Bukharin, was arrested, from the very first moment he confessed his 'mistakes' and claimed absolute fidelity to the Central Committee Party line, which was Stalin's line. This odd game, and some unknown facts, were the probable reasons why Astrov, after being kept for four years in the isolator of Verkhne-Uralsk, was sent, in 1936, to Arkhangelsk and later to Smolensk, to forced residence. In Smolensk he was lecturing in history, and meantime started with his former pupil, Pankratova (now a member of the Presidium of the Supreme Soviet and a member of the Soviet Academy of Sciences) to write the history of the October Revolution, which was afterwards published without official mention of his name.

When Russia was attacked in 1941 he volunteered for the army, but was at first refused. However, through the personal intervention of Malenkov (then Secretary of the Central Committee) he was sent as an officer to the political leadership of an army, where he was in charge of troop entertaining. Against his will he was discharged on the eve of victory, in 1945, and returned to Moscow, where he worked up to 1947 in the State Publishing House for Political and Economic Literature. When the huge wave of arrests in 1947 began, Astrov was among the first to be arrested and charged with indirect terrorism (as were all former Trotskyists and Bukharinists). He was 'sentenced' by the Special Commission to twenty-five years prison isolation.

His family life was another tragedy. He was married when very young, to his first love, also a Bolshevik Party member. In spite of having three daughters, they never had a regular family life: when Astrov was arrested for the first time, his wife, to save the family, had to divorce him, and condemn him. Later, while in Smolensk, she joined him again, but at the beginning of the war she was sent to a job in Leningrad, where she and the youngest daughter died of starvation. When Astrov was arrested for the second time his two daughters (one married to a high-ranking army officer and the second to a former pupil of Astrov, a lecturer in history) renounced him, and in the isolator he never received letters or material help. He still claims to be a true Bolshevik, faithful to the Central Committee line. He hopes one day to be rehabilitated and to finish his days with his grandchildren in Moscow. While in prison (after 1953) he wrote an excellent book dedicated to the Soviet youth. He sent the book to Malenkov and received an answer from the Prison

Department of the M.V.D. that when he had finished his prison term his book might be published.

There were also other interesting cases amongst the Soviet citizens, as, for example, *V. M. Rostov*, aged 74, an old Menshevik, member of the Central Committee from 1905 to 1906, and arrested after the first Revolution in 1907, when he was kept, together with Ordzhonikidze, in the fortress of Schluesselburg until February 1917. After the February Revolution he was first a Commissar of an army and, towards the end of Kerensky's regime, Deputy Minister of Agriculture in his government. In October 1917 he was arrested, but released on a personal order of Lenin, remaining untouched until 1947, when he was arrested and charged with anti-Soviet propaganda, for having quoted in the Soviet Writers' Association that 'Britain is the only true democratic country in the world.' For his age he is in good physical condition and opposed to every pro-Soviet activity.

Then there is *P. A. Orlov*, aged 68, a high-ranking officer from World War I, then fighting in the Civil War against the Bolsheviks. From 1928 until 1941 he was in the Donets Basin under a false name, even becoming a member of the Party Bureau of this area. After the German occupation he joined the Cossack Volunteers and was the Town Major of Krasnodon. (See A. Fadeyev's *The Young Guard*.) In 1945 he was arrested in Austria and sentenced to twenty-five years isolation. In spite of his age, he is still very strong and openly anti-Soviet.

Among the younger Soviet generation there were two cases of heroes of the Soviet Union. The first was a former Major General, *Yegorushkin*, aged 48, a peasant's son, who, in World War II, commanded a division of the Interior Army (M.V.D.). In 1949 he was arrested for alleged anti-Soviet propaganda and was sentenced to ten years prison isolation by the Special Commission. He told me that while he was drunk he had said something stupid about Stalin. He is, on the other hand, a faithful Soviet man, as, for him personally, the regime had done everything. Intellectually not very developed, he could, in Western Europe, easily have been mistaken for an army R.S.M.

The other hero of the Soviet Union was *V. A. Smirnov*, aged 38. Until 1949 he was a shipyard engineer in Koenigsberg. During the last war he had been a pilot and in 1944 was rewarded with the highest Soviet order. While working in Koenigsberg after the war he organized a circle where political, economic and cultural problems of Soviet life were discussed. Arrested in 1949, he was charged with being the organizer of the so-called 'Rabochaya Oppositsiya' (Worker Opposition) and for this activity he was sentenced to twenty-five years' solitary prison isolation. Smirnov changed his mind in prison several times. Generally the Soviet citizens were very careful in their way of speaking: few of them—almost exclusively old people—were anti-Soviet. The majority of them, when talking to foreigners, partially criticized the Soviet regime, but in the presence of other Soviet citizens they never expressed any criticism against the Soviet regime.

For obvious reasons it would be inadvisable for me here to give the names or identifiable details of the foreigners.

I could extend this list of prisoners kept in isolators in Russia, mostly charged with alleged crimes and, according to our Western principles of law, absolutely innocent, but I am not considering it my task, as I think that an international body will some day take charge of this tremendous work. When I left the isolator of Aleksandrovsk in October 1955—officially on the basis of a Supreme Soviet Amnesty, but effectively because of the constant care and pressure of the Western world—I promised myself I would give a message to the world concerning these happenings. And this is part of the picture.

AUTHORS OF PAPERS

E. J. Scott served in the British Embassy in Moscow from 1949 to 1951. From 1951 to 1953 he was engaged in research at St. Antony's College Oxford.

David Footman joined the Levant Consular Service in 1919. On retiring from the Foreign Office in 1953 he became Fellow of St. Antony's College. Author of *Red Prelude*, a study of the Russian Revolutionary movement 1860-81.

Alec Nove is a specialist in the economy of the U.S.S.R. and author of a number of articles. He was a member of the British Agricultural Delegation to Russia in 1955.

Wolfgang Leonhard, born 1922, was taken to the Soviet Union in 1935. He became a Komsomol member and attended the Komintern School near Ufa 1942-3. In April 1945 he was sent to Berlin with Walter Ulbricht. He worked in the Agitprop department of the Central committee of the K.P.D. and S.E.D., and was instructor at the Party Higher School 'Karl Marx' till 1949, when he broke with the East German authorities and left for Belgrade. He is now engaged on a course of study and research at St. Antony's College.

George Sherman is a graduate of Dartmouth College, N.H., and has engaged in post-graduate studies at Columbia University and St. Antony's College, Oxford. He visited the U.S.S.R. in 1955.

Geoffrey Wheeler after serving in the Indian Army and Indian Political Service was Counsellor at the British Embassy in Tehran from 1946 to 1950. He is now Director of the Central Asian Research Centre and joint editor of *The Central Asian Review* (published in association with St. Antony's College).

W. Claudius is a German journalist who was arrested in Berlin in 1950 and held for five years in various prisons in the U.S.S.R. He was released late in 1955 with a number of other German prisoners. He now lives in Western Germany.